THE WORKING LIFE

A Colonial Craftsman

THE WORKING LIFE

A Colonial Craftsman

TITLES IN THE WORKING LIFE SERIES INCLUDE:

An Actor on the Elizabethan Stage

The Cavalry During the Civil War

A Colonial Craftsman

A Renaissance Painter's Studio

A Roman Gladiator

A Roman Senator

A Sweatshop During the Industrial Revolution

A Worker on the Transcontinental Railroad

THE WORKING LIFE

A Colonial Craftsman

MARY C. WILDS

LUCENT BOOKS

An imprint of Thomson Gale, a part of The Thomson Corporation

THOMSON

GALE

Detroit • New York • San Francisco • San Diego • New Haven, Conn. • Waterville, Maine • London • Munich

For more information, contact
Lucent Books
27500 Drake Rd.
Farmington Hills, MI 48331-3535
Or you can visit our Internet site at http://www.gale.com

LIBRARY OF CONGRESS CATALOGING-IN-PUBLICATION DATA

Wilds, Mary, 1960–
    A colonial craftsman/ by Mary C. Wilds.
        p. cm. — (Working life series)
    Includes bibliographical references and index:
    Summary: The lives of those who worked as craftsmen in colonial America: apprentices, blacksmiths, gunsmiths, silversmiths, wigmakers, and printers.
    ISBN 1-59018-176-X (lib.: alk. paper)
    1. Handicraft—United States—History—Juvenile literature. 2. Artisans—United States—History—Juvenile literature. 3. United States—Social life and customs—To 1775—Juvenile literature. I. Title. II. Series.
    TT23.W54 2004
    680'.973—dc022
                                                                    2004010855

Printed in the United States of America

CONTENTS

FOREWORD

"The strongest bond of human sympathy outside the family relations should be one uniting all working people of all nations and tongues and kindreds."

Abraham Lincoln, 1864

Work is a common activity in which almost all people engage. It is probably the most universal of human experiences. As Henry Ford, inventor of the Model T said, "There will never be a system invented which will do away with the necessity of work." For many people, work takes up most of their day. They spend more time with their coworkers than with family and friends. And the common goals people pursue on the job may be among the first thoughts that they have in the morning, and the last that they may have at night.

While the idea of work is universal, the way it is done and who performs it vary considerably throughout history. The story of work is inextricably tied to the history of technology, the history of culture, and the history of gender and race. When the typewriter was invented, for example, it was considered the exclusive domain of men who worked as secretaries. As women workers became more accepted, the secretarial role was gradually filled by women. Finally, with the invention of the computer, the modern secretary spends little time actually typing correspondence. Files are delivered via computer, and more time is spent on other tasks than the manual typing of correspondence and business.

This is just one example of how work brings together technology, gender, and culture. Another example is the American plantation slave. The harvesting of cotton was initially so cumbersome and time consuming that even with slaves its profitability was doubtful. With the invention of the cotton gin, however, efficiency improved, and slavery became a viable agricultural tool. It also became a southern tradition and institution, enough that the South was willing to go to war to preserve it.

The books in Lucent's Working Life series strive to show the intermingling of work, and its reflection in culture, technology, race, and gender. Indeed, history viewed through the perspective of the average worker is both enlightening and fascinating. Take the history of the typewriter, mentioned above. Readers today have access to more technology than any of their historical counterparts, and, in fact, though they would find the typewriter's keyboard familiar, they would find using it a bore. Finding out that people spent their days sitting over that machine (with no talk of carpal tunnel syndrome!) and were valued if they made no typing errors because corrections were cumbersome to make and, in some legal professions, made documents invalid, is an interesting story that involves many different aspects of history.

The desire to work is almost innate. As German socialist Ferdinand Lassalle said in the 1850s, "Workingmen we all are so far as we have the desire to make ourselves useful to human society in any way whatever." Yet each historical period offers a million different stories of the history of each job and how it was performed. And that history is the history of human society.

Each book in the Working Life series strives to tell the tale of these anonymous workers. Primary source quotes offer veracity and immediacy to each volume, letting the workers themselves tell their stories. In addition, thorough bibliographies tell students where they can find out more information, and complete indexes allow for easy perusal of the text. While students learn about the work of years gone by, they gain empathy for those who toil and, perhaps, a universal pride in taking up the work that will someday be theirs.

BUILDING A NEW WORLD

In colonial America nothing was mass-produced. Everything from tools to guns to books was handmade one at a time by craftsmen: blacksmiths, printers, silversmiths, and other professionals. Colonial craftsmen provided the items necessary for everyday life and therefore were indispensable. It was craftsmen who provided the nails to build houses; the wigs that well-dressed men and women wore; the guns a man used for hunting or to protect his family; the array of silver dishes that adorned the homes of wealthy merchants or planters; and the Bibles colonists took with them to church or kept in their homes. The list of what craftsmen made is endless: hammers, horseshoes, candles, barrels, harnesses, pewter tankards, shoes, eyeglasses, plows, cloth, and hats, to name just a few. Some craftsmen, such as the silversmith, were highly esteemed by their fellow colonists, in part because they were considered artists whose works were not just valuable but beautiful. Other craftsmen, like the blacksmith and gunsmith, made more utilitarian items like ax heads and long rifles, but their work was no less vital to the colonists. In certain ways theirs was the more important work, since an ax and a gun would do more to feed a family than a beautiful set of silver could.

All craftsmen were also small businessmen. Unlike unskilled laborers, who had little hope of economic advancement, craftsmen—especially those who were particularly adept—could earn enough to put aside savings for the future. Learning a craft in a growing land like America thus became a way for a poor man to improve his circumstances.

As vital as he was in society, the craftsman was greatly outnumbered in America. Less than 20 percent of colonists worked in a craft. Most colonists were farmers and a few were "gentlemen"—that is, individuals who had inherited wealth or whose positions did not involve physical toil, mostly clergymen and scholars.

THE POLITICAL BACKBONE

Craftsmen were not just vital to physical survival in the colonies. In many ways, they formed the political backbone of colonial communities. Most craftsmen dealt with colonists at every social and economic level: farmers, gentlemen, the poor, and other craftsmen. They were well known to their neighbors, so when the people looked in their midst to elect local leaders, craftsmen often filled these positions. Over time, dissatisfaction grew in the colonies in regard to British policies, such as British taxes and trade rules. As dissatisfaction evolved into agitation and then outright rebellion, it was these individuals who ended up leading the new nation called the United States.

Nevertheless, the world of the craftsman invariably began and ended in his

In this eighteenth-century illustration, colonial craftsmen apply their trades as farmers plow fields outside Boston.

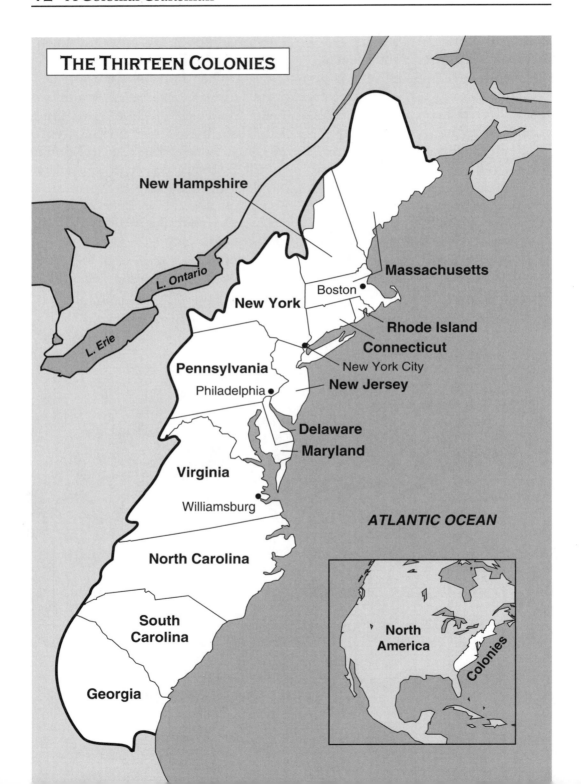

THE THIRTEEN COLONIES

New Hampshire

L. Ontario

L. Erie

Massachusetts

Boston

New York

Rhode Island

Connecticut

New York City

Pennsylvania

New Jersey

Philadelphia

Delaware

Maryland

Virginia

Williamsburg

ATLANTIC OCEAN

North Carolina

South Carolina

North America

Colonies

Georgia

workshop. Some, like the blacksmith, worked virtually alone, save for one or two helpers, and relied on their own skill, physical strength, and dexterity to earn their living. Even in crafts such as the printing trade that did employ many workers and used large and somewhat complex machines, skilled manpower was vital in ensuring the output of a good product, one that would live up to or enhance its creator's reputation. It was in the craftsman's interest, therefore, to hire the best helpers he could.

Those helpers almost always were boys. Indeed, whatever the craft, its practitioners were almost exclusively men. Although women did practice some crafts, such as candle making, within the home, nearly all professional craftsmen were men. Even if a young woman wanted to learn a craft, there was a virtually insurmountable barrier to her doing so: Craftsmen chose who they would take into their workshops for training, and social norms of the day dictated that they choose boys. Part of the craftsman's job, then, was to train both his helpers and his successors. In colonial America, the first step to becoming a craftsman was to work for one.

CHAPTER 1

BECOMING A CRAFTSMAN

Schools for the crafts did not exist in early America. All craftsmen learned by doing, so those who aided a craftsman on a daily basis in his shop—apprentices and journeymen—learned to do what he did by helping him while he worked. Those who actually worked as craftsmen were the only ones who passed on the knowledge and skills of their crafts to a new generation. The craftsman, therefore, doubled as teacher and employer.

The apprentice spent several years in an on-the-job training situation. He lived with the craftsman, worked with him, and was bound by contract not to leave his employ until the contract was up, no matter how unhappy in the situation he might be. The apprentice occupied the lowest position in the social order in a craftsman's shop. Apprentices performed a myriad of small daily tasks, in return for which they received only room and board. Gradu-

ally, an apprentice took on larger tasks and more responsibility as he learned his master's craft.

The road from apprentice status to that of master craftsman could be tedious and trying at times, but it did ensure that those who performed the task of making things that were vital to daily existence knew how to do it well and were ready to pass on their knowledge when the time was right.

GIVING A BOY A FUTURE

A boy in colonial America was considered old enough to become an apprentice around the age of thirteen. When a craftsman was ready to bring a youngster into the shop as an apprentice, he typically signed a contract with the youth's father or guardian. This contract, known as an indenture, bound the boy to work for the craftsman, whom he called his "master," for a period of four to five years. The craftsman was expected to teach, feed, clothe, and house the boy. In return, the youngster was expected to obey his master in all respects and perform whatever task his master required of him. He was also expected to exhibit good moral character and attend church services regularly if his master required it, as most did.

In his book *The Colonial Silversmith*, Henry J. Kauffman excerpts an actual contract between Boston goldsmith Charles Le Roux and his fifteen-year-old apprentice, Jacob Ten Eyck, dated July 23, 1719. This contract lists in great detail how Le Roux expected his new apprentice to behave:

He shall not waste his master's goods nor lend them unlawfully to any. . . . At cards dice or any other unlawful game he shall not play

Apprentices learn to operate looms. Apprenticeships provided colonial boys with opportunities to learn marketable skills.

whereby his master may have damage. . . . He shall not absent himself day nor night from his master's service without his leave not haunt alehouses, taverns or playhouses but in all things as a faithful apprentice he shall behave himself toward his master.[1]

As confining as such terms might have seemed for a teenager, it was in his interests to put up with them.

Learning a craft was virtually the only way that a boy whose family was not wealthy could hope to better his prospects in colonial America. Thus, the master craftsman who took a boy on as an apprentice undoubtedly became the most important adult in his life, except for his own father.

FATHERS KNEW BEST

The youth himself was rarely consulted before the contract was signed. In

In 1717 Benjamin Franklin (center) became an apprentice in his brother's printing shop.

colonial society, a man chose his son's profession, so all the initial dealings between craftsman and apprentice were handled by the boy's father. The boy's own interests and talents were usually not taken into account, though some colonial fathers did try to find a craft that suited their sons' abilities. One such individual was Josiah Franklin, father of Benjamin Franklin. Josiah, a candle maker, shopped around for months to find an appropriate apprenticeship for his son, since Benjamin had shown little talent for making candles. Franklin later remembered, "[My father] sometimes took me to walk with him and see joiners, bricklayers, turners, braziers . . . at their work, [so] that he might observe my inclination, and endeavour to fix it on some trade or other."[2]

Benjamin was eventually bound over to his own brother, James, a printer, in 1717. Father Josiah, Franklin later explained, decided that since Ben so loved to read, the printing trade would suit him best. "This bookish inclination at length determin'd my Father to make me a printer," Franklin recalled. "He had already one son [James] of that profession. In 1717 my brother James returned from England with a press and letters to set up his business in Boston."[3]

TRICKS OF THE TRADE
Once a boy became an apprentice he would never live with his family again.

A room above the master's shop became his home and learning his master's craft became the focus of his life. Master craftsmen usually asked their apprentices to take over the more routine chores in the shop, which gave them time to focus on the more exacting tasks. A master blacksmith, for example, required his apprentice to keep the fires burning in the shop's forge each day so that he could concentrate on heating iron and forging tools.

Having an apprentice was sometimes vital to the success of the craftsman's business. A wig maker's day was spent dealing with customers and creating products so he had little time for necessary tasks such as wig deliveries. Any boy apprenticed to a wig maker spent a good portion of his workweek delivering finished wigs to his master's customers, as one colonial writer observed:

> On a Saturday afternoon, it was not unusual to see scores of wigmakers apprentices dashing through the narrow streets of Boston, or any other early American city, rushing to deliver the freshly curled and powdered wigs belonging to the great and near great men of the day.[4]

LEARNING THE CRAFT
The apprentice began learning some of his master's skills gradually, taking on a new assignment only when his master deemed him ready. These

assignments were attempted under the master's close supervision. The blacksmith, for example, brought along his apprentice when he went to a customer's barn to shoe horses. Once there, he expected his apprentice to restrain each horse while he inspected the animal's hooves and shoes. After several such excursions the youth would be asked to actually shoe a horse, with his master's supervision. The actual forging of horseshoes required experience and skill, so the smith would never ask a green apprentice to join him at the forge and actually pound metal into shape. Later on, as he became more experienced at the forge, the smith's apprentice would take on the making of the shoe itself.

❧ ORPHANS AND THE ❧ APPRENTICE SYSTEM

Orphaned or indigent boys were considered the responsibility of their community in colonial America. Rather than allow the youths to fend for themselves, community leaders often stepped in to pair a parentless boy with a master craftsman who needed help. In addition, poor families were often pressured to apprentice their children at a very early age; this was considered one of the best ways to lead a youth out of poverty. Printer Isaiah Thomas is an extreme example, having been apprenticed to a Boston printer when he was only six years old. Thomas's father had abandoned him, and his mother, having no way to support her son, agreed to the apprenticeship despite the fact that most apprenticeships at the time began when a youth was thirteen.

Thomas's master immediately put him to work cleaning the workshop and handling other tasks. He even built a special bench so that the diminutive Thomas could reach the shelf where the lead type was kept. As Joseph Blumenthal records in *The Printed Book in America*, Thomas later wrote of his experiences as an apprentice: "After I was bound and he [Zechariah Fowle] had absolute power over me, he . . . placed me at the type cases. In order that I might reach the boxes of both capitals and lower cases [of type] he had a bench made of sufficient heighth, and of the length of a double frame."

Thomas went on to excel in his craft. He started his own newspaper, the *Massachusetts Spy*, when he was only twenty years old. He also became a historian, bound and printed books, made his own paper, and operated a bookstore. He was also a vocal supporter of the American Revolution.

Wig makers, too, delegated tasks to an apprentice as soon as the youth was ready. One of the earliest tasks a boy learned to assume was the shaving of a customer's beard, since wig makers doubled as barbers. Colonial men customarily went clean shaven. Once a week the wealthiest among them, instead of shaving themselves, paid for a shave by the local wig maker. Wig makers also shaved customers' heads when a wig was ready for the final fitting; this task, too, invariably fell to an apprentice.

LIVING CONDITIONS AND EDUCATION

Since apprentices were not paid and could not legally leave their masters' employ, some modern observers have characterized the apprentice system as short-term slavery. However, most colonial masters would have considered themselves more of a surrogate parent than a slaveholder. Some of them even took it upon themselves to educate their charges, holding reading, writing, and math classes in the shop at the end of the day after the work was done. Most masters, however, did not have time to be a schoolteacher as well as an employer and preferred to let those apprentices who wanted a formal education seek it on their own.

If an apprentice decided to attend school, he had to do so on his own time. Most towns had evening schools, which apprentices usually attended since they were obligated to work for their masters during the day. Similarly, it was up to the apprentice or his family to pay for such schooling. Colonial schools were not paid for by taxpayers, and few, if any, masters were willing to pay the tuition.

Evening school was far different than day school. Day students studied such subjects as Latin and Greek in prepation for studying law or becoming clergymen. Evening students took more practical courses. For example, evening students would not study a foreign language, but they would learn to survey property and add and subtract columns of figures.

WHEN APPRENTICES WENT MISSING

Because boys were apprenticed at such a young age and usually were given little choice as to what profession they might enter, it is not surprising that some became dissatisfied with their situation and chose to run away. Colonial newspapers were full of advertisements by craftsmen who were seeking help in tracking down a runaway apprentice. Such ads were rarely complimentary to the youth in question. One published in New York in the 1730s, for example, described the missing teen as "pretty much pitted with the small pox, wears his own hair [meaning that he did not wear a wig, as many colonists did], and is much

R UN away, the 23d of this Inftant *January*, from *Silas Crifpin* of *Burlington*, Taylor, a Servant Man na-med *Jofeph Morris*, by Trade a Taylor, aged about 22 Years, of a middle Sta-ture, fwarthy Complexion, light gray Eyes, his Hair clipp'd off, mark'd with a large pit of the Small Pox on one Cheek near his Eye, had on when he went away a good Felt Hat, a yelowifh Drugget Coat with Pleits behind, an old Ozenbrigs Veft, two Ozenbrigs Shirts, a pair of Leather Breeches handfomely worm'd and flower'd up the Knees, yarn Stockings and good round toe'd Shoes   Took with him a large pair of Sheers crack'd in one of the Bows, & mark'd with the Word [*Savoy*].   Whoever takes up the faid Servant, and fecures him fo that his Mafter may have him again, fhall have *Three Pounds* Reward befides reafo-nable Charges,   paid by me   *Silas Crifpin.*

An advertisement offers a reward for the return of a runaway servant. Although most apprentices enjoyed their positions, some ran away from their masters.

bloated by drinking, to which he is most uncommonly addicted."[5]

Esther Forbes, in her biography of silversmith Paul Revere, *Paul Revere and the World He Lived In*, put the blame for runaways on both sides. Craftsmen, after all, were known to beat their apprentices, though never on the Sabbath, Forbes points out. And a youthful apprentice was at the mercy of his master; if the craftsman starved him or did not buy him new shoes for the winter, the apprentice had little recourse, since he was legal-ly bound to the man until his term of service was up. On the other hand, apprentices could be difficult to control, partly because of their age. As Forbes explains, "[Apprentices] worked hours that would supposedly kill a modern boy and had often too much energy left over. They lied . . . they left care-less fires . . . they stole great wigs and silver spoons. They ran away and were whipped publicly and privately."[6]

It is impossible to know what became of most runaways. Some were undoubtedly found and returned to their masters; others may have found another type of work in a different city. Most apprentices, however, did not run away. Most were treated well enough by their masters that they chose to stay with them, even after they graduated to the rank of journeyman.

BECOMING A JOURNEYMAN

A journeyman was a craftsman who had passed through the apprenticeship phase successfully but was not yet financially ready to open his own shop. The journeyman worked for the master craftsman for pay, honing and perfecting the skills he had learned during his apprenticeship. Since he was an employee, not the shop owner, the journeyman had no say in how business was conducted or how the product was sold or produced. Unlike the apprentice, however, he was free to find a new job if he was unhappy in his current situation. Many young colonial craftsmen did just that, earning the name "journeymen" since they journeyed from shop to shop and employer to employer. This journeying could last for months or years, until the young craftsman earned enough money to open his own shop.

An apprentice usually passed into the journeyman stage when, after a period of four or five years, his master asked him to present what was called an "apprentice piece" for inspection. This piece, of course, depended on the craft itself: A wig maker's apprentice would create a wig; a blacksmith's apprentice might forge the head of an ax or a hammer; the pewterer would make a plate or cup; and so forth. If

❧ THE ❧ FREEDOM SUIT

One of the most important days in a craftsman's career was the day he received his freedom suit. The suit, which the young man would more likely wear to church or on another formal occasion rather than in his shop, was both a symbol and a rite of passage: He was leaving boyhood and apprenticeship behind and entering the world of adult craftsmen. A freedom suit that once belonged to Jonathan Sheldon of Newport, in the colony of Rhode Island, is now in the permanent possession of the Smithsonian Museum in Washington. Sheldon had been apprenticed to a noted cabinetmaker in Newport and received the suit from him. Made from linen, Sheldon's buttoned jacket and knee breeches are well preserved and fairly typical of the period. Unadorned, simply styled, and sewn for a slender man only five feet tall, the clothes provide some insight into how one American craftsman lived. The clothes are in good condition, indicating that Sheldon took great pains to make sure his freedom suit lasted a lifetime.

the apprentice piece passed inspection, the master craftsman would do two things. He would sign off on the indenture, meaning that the youth, usually by that time about nineteen years old, was free to leave his shop and go work elsewhere for wages if he wished. He also gave his former apprentice a new suit of clothes, a tradition known as "custom of the country" or the "freedom suit," to mark his transition to journeyman.

Colonial accounts do not indicate how often apprentices failed to produce an acceptable apprentice piece, and whether the master himself was held responsible for such a failure. However, although the colonies suffered from a chronic labor shortage and skilled craftsmen were in demand, the master craftsman undoubtedly felt pressured by his community and his peers to turn out the best journeymen possible. A craftsman with an unskilled apprentice or clumsy journeyman was more likely to turn out subpar product. Since his reputation was at times the most valuable asset he had, the craftsman undoubtedly took great pains to protect it by taking on, and turning out, the best help possible.

Depending on the master's needs, a young journeyman might remain in the shop where he had learned his craft or go elsewhere, working for pay wherever he went. That pay, writes Edwin Tunis in *Colonial Craftsmen and the Beginnings of American Industry*, re-mained fairly steady throughout the eighteenth century, despite the chronic labor shortage. In 1760, Tunis says, the average wage for all trades was about 15 shillings a week; this comes out to about $20.50 in today's money.

To earn this wage, journeymen typically worked six days a week, twelve to sixteen hours a day. Some of them used their newfound freedom to travel the colonies, stopping to work whenever and wherever they ran out of funds. Usually craftsmen hired only one or two journeymen in addition to an apprentice, but those who enjoyed a particularly lucrative business took on several. Holding on to good help was one of the greatest challenges a master craftsman faced. Good journeymen were so scarce that craftsmen often stole away each other's help. Rival craftsmen often conducted a war of words in the local newspapers, each accusing the other of nefarious deeds and unfair practices.

THE TASKS OF A JOURNEYMAN

Journeymen were skilled laborers, meaning that they could handle projects with minimal supervision, often from start to finish. However, the master craftsman was still responsible for every product that came out of his shop. Everything he sold had his name on it, so he could not afford to allow even his most talented journeyman to work wholly unsupervised.

Colonial reenactors playing a blacksmith and his journeyman forge a tool. Journeymen were skilled laborers who worked under the direct supervision of their master.

In fact, most master craftsmen had a side-by-side relationship with their journeymen. The master blacksmith, for example, required his journeyman to handle the physical labor while a tool was forged, yet the smith himself made all the decisions as to how the tool would be shaped and finished. The pair would heat metal in the shop's forge and then place it on the huge anvil that served as the smith's primary tool. The smith held the iron in place, and the journeyman took on the role of striker, meaning that he struck the metal with a heavy hammer, laying blows wherever the smith directed him to do so.

Aldren A. Watson, in his book *The Village Blacksmith*, describes this process in great detail:

By lightly tapping the spot with his small hammer, the blacksmith showed his striker where he wanted the sledge to strike. A good striker was expected to use the sledge [hammer] left or right-handed with equal ease, delivering the blows from any angle and

❧ A LABOR SHORTAGE ❧

The colonies suffered from such a chronic labor shortage that master craftsmen frequently looked abroad for labor, since training their own help often took too much time. They might either hire a journeyman who recently arrived from Europe or recruit skilled labor via their overseas contacts. Craftsmen took care to let current and prospective customers know that they hired only the most talented journeymen. In a 1746 newspaper advertisement, Williamsburg wig maker Andrew Finnie boasted that he had just imported from London a new shipment of wigmaking materials and "some exceeding good workmen." As the pamphlet *The Wigmaker in Eighteenth-Century Williamsburg* reports, Finnie's advertisement concluded, "As I have a great many good Workmen, Gentlemen and others may depend on being speedily and faithfully served, in the best manner."

placing them with unfailing accuracy on the head of the tool the blacksmith held. He had to hold to a regular rhythm and keep his eyes open; when the smith tapped a different spot, or rotated the work on the anvil, the striker was to be ready for just a momentary pause and then a full-sized blow.[7]

Even though the journeyman was responsible for the blows that shaped the piece during this process, the master still determined its shape and design. All but the least ambitious journeymen longed for this type of control and diligently saved their wages until they, too, could open their own shops. Only those who had a business of their own and a product with their name on it could be called master craftsmen.

The journeyman who managed to finally open his own shop would, in a real sense, have the opportunity to become one of the colony's leading citizens. And because of the nature of his trade, one of the most prominent of a colony's citizens was bound to be the blacksmith.

CHAPTER 2

THE BLACKSMITH

More than forty crafts were practiced in the American colonies during the years leading up to the Revolutionary War. Among the craftsmen whose work was most in demand, however, was the blacksmith.

"The blacksmith was early recognized as one tradesman who was almost indispensable to the survival of the community," Watson writes. "In fact, of all the artisans, the smith possibly answered the greatest number of villagers' needs. Every one of his neighbors needed something made of iron, whether for the farm, the sawmill, the woods, or the granite quarry."[8]

"The blacksmith executed nearly all early ironwork," adds Scott G. Williamson in his book *The American Craftsman*. "The blacksmith made . . . latches, hinges, gates, fences, andirons and similar objects. He was also the general maker of tools"[9] for himself, his neighbors, and his fellow craftsmen. Since every colonist, rich or poor, needed iron implements of some sort, the blacksmith invariably worked with all levels of society. He made pots and kettles for the housewife, field hoes for the farmer, and chandeliers for the tavern owner. If he lived in a port town or city, he more than likely supplied the ironwork used by shipbuilders and whalers. Watson explains: "[Blacksmiths] were forging anchor chains, bolts, eyes and scores of special fittings for [America's] shipyards. The growing whaling industry had its own blacksmiths, turning out harpoon heads, cutting blades, and other [tools] necessary for killing whales."[10]

The blacksmith was also an important supplier for his fellow craftsmen since he made the ironwork they needed to complete their own products. For example, if a carriage maker required

A contemporary painting depicts a blacksmith and his apprentice in their forge. The work of the blacksmiths was indispensable to the survival of colonial communities.

a set of iron steps to complete a buggy he was making, he would ask the local blacksmith to craft those for him at his forge.

Blacksmithing was one of the most physically demanding of all the crafts. The blacksmith spent his days over a hot forge, wielding heavy hammers as he shaped hot iron into water dippers, horseshoes, sled runners, or any other product his customers requested. He combined heat and precise hammer blows as he worked to bend iron into any number of shapes. His shop was often so noisy from hammering that he and his helpers could communicate only via hand signals. The steady, regular hammering in the blacksmith's shop could be felt in the ground around the anvil and heard a mile away from the shop. And since the smith was working with iron heated to 400 degrees Fahrenheit and beyond, his shop was undoubtedly an uncomfortable place to work.

Yet a blacksmith must have gained much satisfaction from creating such a wide variety of products so important to his community. True, he was not considered an artist in the way that a goldsmith or silversmith was; unlike them, the blacksmith did not sign his work. But since most of his products were meant to be used in everyday life, his work had an impact on the well-being of his neighbors. It is not surprising, then, that in most communities the blacksmith's shop became a

melting pot for people from all walks of life. As they gathered there they would debate local issues, gossip, and even horse trade while they waited to speak to the smith.

For his part, the blacksmith worked hard to please his customers. Most of his products were custom-made, meaning that he made every ax head, kettle, and andiron when his customer requested it, usually tailoring the piece to that customer's specifications. Only a few products, such as nails, would he make and sell in quantity.

IRON FOR THE FORGE

No matter what the product, the blacksmith always worked in iron. The earliest colonial blacksmiths imported their iron from Europe. There were no colonial ironworks, or processing plants, to fall back on because early settlers did not build them. The first colonists were more interested in building settlements than searching the hills and bogs around them for iron ore. Most colonial iron originated in Russia or Sweden and was shipped by way of Britain, so it was very expensive. Such shiploads of iron spent months at sea, often with long delays, invariably further inflating costs.

Expensive iron made for expensive products, so colonists eventually began to search out iron deposits closer to home. Iron ore deposits proved most plentiful in the colonies of Virginia, Vermont, Maryland, Connecticut, and New Hampshire. Ironworks turned the ore into iron bars by smelting it in a furnace. The iron bars would then be transported to customers and the blacksmiths by horse and wagon.

TOOLS OF THE TRADE

The smith would spent twelve to fourteen hours a day in his workshop, which was called a smithy, turning the iron into various products for customers. The most important place in any smithy was its forge. Made of brick and built atop a stone foundation, the forge's square brick chimney vented smoke through the roof throughout the day. When building his forge, the smith would place a leather bellows behind the chimney and attach it to an air pipe that vented the smoke into the outdoors. The bellows was used to help start the fire in the morning. If ever the fire burned low during the day, the blacksmith would instruct his apprentice to pump the bellows again, since a fresh burst of oxygen would revive the fire.

The smith kept a flat table beside the hearth on which he would lay pieces of iron to be forged that day. Beside the hearth and table would be the anvil. Heavy and fixed in place, the anvil had to be able to absorb many blows from a hammer. Thus, the smith would mount and secure his anvil on a post that was buried four or five feet in the ground. This ensured that the anvil would remain firmly anchored through years of work.

AT THE FORGE

The blacksmith's work was difficult and precise. Watson explains:

> [The blacksmith's] work demanded a sense of timing, and a kind of resolution that separated him from other men who worked with their hands. His . . . raw material was not static like wood and leather. His iron had a life of its own, and its behavior obliged him to make his decisions instantly. No other workman was required to carry out his tasks with such rapid-fire movements.[11]

Before this intense work could begin, however, the morning fire had to be lit. The first part of this job usually fell to the apprentice. He would get up early, split some pine and oak logs from a woodpile the smith kept outside his workshop, and then bring in kindling and some wood shavings. The master smith built the fire himself. He would clean out the previous day's ashes, pack the forge with wood shavings, and then pile up the kindling in such a way that there would be plenty of air pockets between the logs. After he lit the fire, he would rake some charcoal into the forge to ensure that it burned bright. When the time was right, he would pump the bellows until the coals burned white and red. The smith used the bellows sparingly throughout the day, since too much oxygen would eat up the charcoal.

❧ MINING AMERICAN IRON ❧

The earliest blacksmiths imported iron from England, but colonists soon learned to dig ore from surface mines in the hills or from the iron ore deposits that formed in lowland swamps. Ironworks, which extracted iron from the ore by smelting it in a furnace, had sprung up in the colonies by 1722. Domestic sales of iron that was mined and processed in America gradually overtook sales of iron imports. This turn of events dismayed the British Crown, which collected taxes on any material imported to the colonies. The Crown attempted to discourage colonists from buying American iron products and American blacksmiths from making them. These restrictions extended to other crafts, and the ensuing conflict was one of many that led to the American War of Independence.

A fire would burn all day long in the forge, since the smith heated his raw material as much as four or five times during the course of his work. When iron is heated to very high temperatures, it becomes soft and malleable. The smith would shape the iron when it was in that state. But if it cooled off before he was finished shaping the piece, he would have to take it back to the forge and heat it again.

When the fire was ready and the blacksmith ready to go to work, he would don a leather apron he kept near the forge; the apron protected his body from the sparks that were generated by his pounding on the hot metal. He would also assemble the array of tools he would use frequently throughout the day. These included the tongs he used to hold the iron in the fire and different-sized hammers, rasps, and files.

Once all the tools were in place, he would take hold of the iron bar with the tongs and hold it in the fire. He would begin working with the metal after it reached a certain temperature. Since iron changes color as it heats, the smith would wait for a certain color to appear as he held the piece in the fire. His experience would have taught him which "color" was best. According to historical records of that period, the colonial blacksmith often preferred his piece to turn lemon yellow before he took it out of the fire and went to work at the anvil; yellow apparently signaled the correct temperature for many jobs. In *The Village Blacksmith*, Watson describes what the smith saw while he waited:

At first the iron looked dull red, but as its temperature increased its color changed to cherry red, then

Blacksmiths forge ax heads in a colonial tool shop. Axes were among the blacksmith's most important creations.

to yellow, and finally to forging color—a bright lemon yellow. Now was the moment to take it out of the fire before it reached white heat, for at that nearly fluid stage it would easily burn.[12]

THE SMITH AT WORK

The blacksmith produced a variety of vital items and performed tasks that required diverse tools and procedures. Ax heads were among the most important products he made; colonists depended on axes for chopping firewood and to fell the trees they used to build their homes, public buildings, and livestock pens. The smith began the process of making an ax by heating two flat pieces of iron that were approximately the same size. Once they were hot, he would insert a thin, cold piece of iron between them and pound one side of the hot metal until both edges merged into one. He would then hammer the other side, reheat it, then hammer again until that side was a flat blade. Finally, the smith would pound out the center iron, leaving behind the hole that eventually would accommodate the ax handle.

❧ AN AMERICAN AX ☙

The colonial blacksmith, using advice from his customers, developed a type of ax head unique to the American colonies. The American ax differed from its European predecessors in that its poll, the flat side of the blade, was heavier than its sharpened side. Moreover, the ax's cutting edge was straight, rather than fashioned in an arc, as European axes were.

There are a number of theories as to why the ax developed in this fashion. Blacksmiths were known to tailor products to their customers' needs, and historians believe that many American settlers, inexperienced with axes, found it difficult to fell trees with a conventionally styled tool. So blacksmiths made the ax blade thinner by grinding it on the grindstone. When an ax poll was heavier than its sharp blade, the settler was able to swing a straighter stroke and thus able to chop in a smoother fashion.

The so-called American ax became the favorite of both inexperienced and experienced woodsmen. America was a rough, wild country that needed to be tamed, and even the strongest and surest of men wanted the best tool possible for doing the taming. Writes Scott G. Williamson in his book *The American Craftsman*, "[The ax] must be set down as one of the first great communal inventions of America due, not so much to our inexperience, as to the fact that we were confronted with more unfelled trees than any other people in civilized times."

In this nineteenth-century woodcut, a farmer fells trees with an American ax, a tool invented by colonial blacksmiths.

The smith would utilize a different set of tools while making a door hinge, another common product. While making the hinge, the smith placed the hot metal between two tools known as fullering irons. Fullering irons were heavy, unheated iron wedges used to flatten a piece of iron. He would instruct his helper, the striker, to pound the fullering irons with a sledgehammer until the iron between them grew long and thin. When the iron was ready, the smith took over. He would flatten the hinge even further with a special hammer that was almost entirely flat on one side. Once this part of the job was finished, the smith used a punch to make holes in one side of the hinge. A punch was a hammer that was flat on one end of the head and shaped to a point at the other. With help from a journeyman the smith held the punch in place, pointed side down, and drilled it through the metal by pounding the flat side with a second hammer.

The smith's helper was indispensable when it came to heavier pieces such as sled runners and wagon axles. For these products the smith would begin with one of his largest pieces of iron. The smith and his striker would carry the iron together to the fire, heat it to its proper temperature, and take it to the anvil. They then worked as a team, the smith tapping the metal with a small hammer to let the striker know where to land his blows and whether to strike a heavy blow or a light one.

The rhythmic hammering of the smith and his striker was well known in colonial towns and villages, historians say. The tap of the smith's hammer would alternate with the striker's heavy, sledgehammer blows, creating a rhythm that could be felt in the ground near the shop and heard up to a mile away.

TEMPERING IRON

Tempering the iron was every bit as important as shaping it. If left untempered, an iron tool might crack or break while in use. When a smith tempered iron, he heated and cooled it in rapid succession, a technique that hardened the metal until it was strong but not brittle. A properly tempered tool could withstand years of use and all types of weather and conditions.

Tempering was both necessary and demanding. The smith relied on his years of experience to judge how long to leave whatever he was making in the fire before cooling it. He had no temperature gauge by which to ascertain how hot the metal had become, so instead he watched the metal change color. The smith would wait until the metal turned cherry red before pulling it from the forge.

The tempering process mostly involved waiting for the iron to heat and then to cool. Watson describes a smith at work, leaning over the hot forge and watching carefully as an iron ladle went back into the flames: "The heat-treated [ladle] was once more put into the fire and allowed to soak up heat slowly until about two inches of the tip was a bright cherry red. Then it was immediately quenched [in water]."[13]

The tempering process was not finished after only one or two rounds. Most tools, including a ladle, required several trips to the forge and bucket before the tempering was complete. Thus, while tempering his ladle, the

A blacksmith heats an iron tool while tempering it. Tempering the iron by heating and cooling it in rapid succession makes the metal strong but not brittle.

❧ SHOEING SAFELY ❧

The colonial blacksmith became quite inventive when it came to shoeing and calming skittish horses and oxen. At times he served as an animal psychologist, talking to it and patting it frequently so that the animal would not be startled if he had to change positions. If the animal had never been shod before, an older animal might be brought along as a companion. The two would be tied and shod side by side, and the presence of the older animal would calm the young one. If this failed to work, a tool called a twitch was applied. The twitch, a short stick with a rope looped through the end, was slipped over the animal's upper lip and twisted, forcing it to stand still.

Horses or oxen who kicked would find one of their feet rendered immobile with a rope; having only three feet ready to kick with usually convinced the animal to stand still while the smith worked. The most difficult animals would be trussed in a canvas sling. The sling was slipped under the animal's belly and then hoisted up, with the help of the farmer and the smith's helpers, until the animal's feet barely touched the floor. In such a position the recalcitrant animal could not struggle and the smith could finish his job in peace.

Blacksmiths shoe a horse. Colonial blacksmiths devised a number of safeguards to ensure their safety while shoeing.

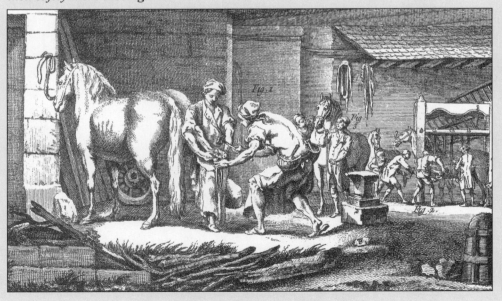

smith repeated the process over and over again, holding the ladle in the flames and then dousing it in water until he was satisfied that the metal was both hard and sturdy. He then completed the process by giving it a final cooling. This time he plunged it deep into the bucket, swishing it about to ensure even and complete cooling.

MAKING HORSESHOES

The smith spent much of his time making, and applying, horseshoes. Horses were indispensable in colonial days, but without something to protect their hooves, the animals would quickly go lame. This protection came in the form of iron "shoes" nailed to the bottom of the horse's hooves. The smith had a time-honored technique for making shoes that rarely varied, Watson says: "The smith's rule was to cut a length of iron about equal to twice the width of the horse's foot at its widest part, twice the thickness of the hoof wall, and the same width as the thickness of the hoof where it touched the ground."[14]

The shoe iron was heated and bent into a curve. The smith heated it a second time and hammered it over the smaller end of the anvil, which was called the horn, until the two ends curved and formed the shape of a half-oval. When the shoe was ready for finishing, the smith forged a flange (or cat's ear, as it was called) on the front part to protect the hoof's front. This step was accomplished by heating the upper part of the shoe once again, placing it on the anvil, and bending the upper half of the shoe to form the flange into a clip with blows from the hammer. While the shoe was still hot the smith would finish it by punching eight holes along its curve, using what was called a blunt punch to mark out the location of the holes and a rectangular punch to drill them out.

THE WANT OF A NAIL

Just as important as the horseshoe itself was the nail used to secure it to the hoof. This was the smith's most common product and also his simplest. Of course, the nail had many uses beyond securing horseshoes: It was used in the building of all sorts of wooden structures, including houses, taverns, barns, and meeting houses, to name just a few. "The demand [for nails] was great and filling it was profitable slack-time work as well as good practice for the apprentices," Edwin Tunis writes. "Making a nail took much less time than it takes to read about it." The smith, or his apprentice, began the process of making a nail by taking in hand a five-foot-long iron rod, anywhere from an eighth to a quarter-inch thick. He would heat one end of the rod and lay it on the anvil. Tunis continues:

> Using the flat face of his hammer, he tapered an inch of the end of the rod, usually on all four sides. . . .

Turning the hammer, he used the sharp peen to cut the rod part way through and then jammed the new point into the tapered hole in the back of his anvil. He snapped the rod off at the cut as soon as the point stuck in the hole. The blunt end of the nail, still hot, stood about a quarter of an inch above the face of an anvil, and the [smith] battered it into a quite large and irregular convex head with a couple of hammer blows.[15]

THE SMITH AS ARTIST

Not all the smith's products were simple and practical. The wrought iron gates, fences, railings, and balconies so popular in colonial cities, particularly in the South, were all made by blacksmiths. This sort of work allowed the smith to express his artistic side. A forged iron hammer or plow only had to be strong and functional, but the iron gate at the entranceway of a planter's home was a symbol of its owner's wealth and status in the community. Hence, the gate, unlike the hammer, had to be impressive and attractive to the eye. So when the smith made these objects, he took care to forge them in a way that made them beautiful as well as durable.

The demand for ornamental iron grew along with the colonies. Most cities and larger towns lit their streets at night with fixed iron lanterns, all of which were made by blacksmiths. Tavern owners, public officials, and planters commissioned smiths to make large iron chandeliers for use in their homes or buildings. Even farmers who did not consider themselves wealthy commissioned blacksmiths to make iron weather vanes for their barns and homes. Such weather vanes, forged in the shape of roosters, horses, and other animals, made for striking silhouettes as one traveled through the colonial countryside.

When he forged a piece of ornamental iron, the smith called on specific skills, just as he did when making an ax or a horseshoe. He began by holding the iron in the fire until the metal turned white hot. At this temperature it was so soft it was almost fluid, this enabled the smith to curl it into spirals, ovals, scrolls, leaves, flowers, and other designs popular in the colonial era.

Ornamental ironwork of the colonial period was graced with all manner of decoration. But most of this work, no matter how beautiful, remained unsigned, for unlike his fellow craftsman, the silversmith, the blacksmith rarely signed his work or even marked it with a distinguishing stamp. Then again, almost everything he made was to be used; even a beautifully wrought chandelier had its function, since it brought light to the great room or dining area in a large building in the evenings.

The ornately decorated iron gate to the colonial governor's mansion in Williamsburg, Virginia, was designed to reflect the governor's status.

THE SMITH IN SOCIETY

The blacksmith's living situation tended to determine the nature of his business. The country blacksmith was truly a generalist; he made everything from household utensils to hoes and plowshares. Often, a rural community had only one blacksmith. He enjoyed the kind of social status that only a lack of competition could bestow.

Urban blacksmiths faced a different situation, however. There tended to be several of them living and working within the town or city limits, so to survive, each smith learned how to specialize. For example, if one smith shod horses, his neighbor might specialize in carriage steps and sled runners, while the smith down the street specialized in household items.

But no matter what his specialty, the blacksmith always seemed to earn respect from his neighbors as an honest, indispensable craftsman. American poet Henry Wadsworth Longfellow would later immortalize the American blacksmith as "a giant of a man in flesh and spirit, once a pillar of society, has become almost a legend."[16] Undoubtedly many of his fellow Americans agreed with him.

CHAPTER 3

THE GUNSMITH

The gunsmith employed techniques similar to the blacksmith's, but he focused on only one product: firearms. In fact, many gunsmiths began their careers in blacksmithing, but as the demand for guns, and gun repair, outstripped demand for other products in their communities, they narrowed their focus.

The colonist's gun was vital to his survival. He used it to protect his family from hostile Indians, to provide meat for his dinner table, and much later, to fight for American independence. The man who forged his gun, therefore, became an important part of the colonial community. In time, American gun makers would also be celebrated for their innovations, particularly for the making and design of the Kentucky rifle, America's first great gun.

Even though he made only one product, the gunsmith was among the most versatile craftsmen in the colonies. He worked with iron, just as the blacksmith did, while making the barrel of a gun. But later in the gun-making process he would work with wood, carving the stock, or handheld portion, of the gun by hand. Finally, if his customer wanted the gun decorated with silver, which many did, he would take on the role of silversmith, creating patterns that made the firearm not just a means of putting food on the table but a work of art. Therefore, a gunsmith had to call on many skills as he worked.

Gunsmiths worked everywhere in the colonies. They could be found in both rural communities and urban settings, but the largest concentration of them settled in the interior regions of Pennsylvania, most notably Lancaster, which had a large German-speaking population. Many German gunsmiths who had immigrated to the New World

A colonist's gun was vital to his survival. In this painting, a father uses his rifle to protect his family as they flee from a Native American attack.

settled in Lancaster so they could live among their countrymen.

During the earliest colonial years, firearms were imported, mostly from England. At first, then, the gunsmith spent most of his workday repairing rather than making firearms. Many supplemented their incomes by forging small items, like shoe buckles and bells, and repairing iron tools made by their fellow craftsmen, blacksmiths.

But as colonial populations grew and settlers continued to move westward, the demand for firearms grew so fast that European gunsmiths could not keep up. Moreover, the need was for weapons more suited to the lifestyle of a woodsman. Gunsmiths now began to concentrate on designing and making their own version of the long rifle, a weapon that was accurate, powerful, and, above all, affordable.

American long rifles became known for their velocity and accuracy. Those who handled them also became known for their skill. One of England's finest marksmen of the day, George Hanger, spoke admiringly of American guns and the skill of those who handled them: "I never saw better rifles (or men that shot them better) than in America."[17]

The men who made these rifles combined both heavy labor and fine craftsmanship during the course of their day. The gunsmith required brute strength, just as the blacksmith did, because he had to hammer and bend iron to form a gun barrel. He worked in a hot, sometimes smoky environment that had to be kept well ventilated during the day, as the fire in the shop's forge burned.

Yet the gunsmith also relied on patience and a good eye for detail as he ground and bored away imperfections when the barrel was completed. He carved the stock from wood in a long, laborious process that also required attention to detail, and finished it with a stain that made his product not just more attractive but more water resistant, which was important on the frontier. And finally, he had to call on his artistic sense as he devised the gun's silver ornamentation. With such fine detail work to attend to, the smith also kept his shop well lit; he usually took care to work in a room with plenty of windows, which were positioned to let in a good deal of natural light.

A PART OF DAILY LIFE

The gun maker's products were a part of daily life in colonial America. Although most colonists were farmers and therefore capable of growing their own food, they still depended on wild game as a regular part of their diet. Colonists hunted deer, bear, or panther for meat, as Hans Tanner notes in *Guns of the World:*

> This was all virgin or sparsely settled territory and . . . [the gun] was even more important than the axe. It was the means of supplying food and buckskin [the cloth of the frontier] for clothing. It provided protection from dangerous animals and hostile Indians. The gunmaker became a very important and respected [member of] the pioneer settlements.[18]

IN THE WORKSHOP

The level of demand for his product dictated the amount of help the gunsmith needed. If a gunsmith operated a small shop in a small community, he usually worked alone or with a journeyman and apprentice. In even more remote areas, gun repairs and orders for new guns would be infrequent enough that the gunsmith could keep up with the demand on his own, with minimal help. But as an area became more populated the gunsmith might have more work than he could handle,

❧ THE SNIPER'S WEAPON ❧

The Kentucky rifle is still considered the colonial gunsmith's greatest achievement. But its very name is a bit of a misnomer, since the rifle was believed to have been developed in Lancaster, Pennsylvania, or possibly Maryland, Virginia, or North Carolina. Historians believe the rifle got its name became of its association with the frontier and Kentucky territory. Explorers like Daniel Boone carried the rifles with them as they pressed westward along the Wilderness Trail into Kentucky.

The gun had its beginnings in the give-and-take between the gunsmith and his customer. Together they developed a firearm that was portable, used less powder and a smaller rifle ball than more conventional weapons, made less noise, held steadier than the older-style musket, and was infinitely more accurate.

European marksmen traditionally loaded their hunting rifles by hammering the bullet in place with an iron loading rod. American gun owners, and presumably their gunsmiths, came up with the idea of wrapping the rifle ball in a greased patch. The ball encased in greased leather or muslin could be loaded in the gun by hand. Unlike the European method, this kind of loading took only a few minutes. The patch enabled the rifle ball to slide easily into the gun. It gave the bullet a good seal and increased its velocity by maintaining good pressure in the barrel. The patch also cleaned the barrel as the bullet propelled through it.

The Kentucky rifle proved most useful in the guerrilla warfare that was such an important part of the American Revolution. Because of its accuracy, it was the gun of choice for snipers and bands of soldiers intent on surprise attacks. On October 7, 1780, nine hundred men armed with Kentucky rifles crept up on a British regiment commanded by Major Patrick Ferguson at King's Mountain, North Carolina. In the ensuing battle the British saw 242 men killed or wounded and 664 captured. In contrast, there were only 28 American deaths and just 90 wounded. This defeat broke the back of British power in the South.

particularly if he was the only gunsmith in town. His workforce would grow along with his shop. In a large shop, the process of making guns took on an assembly-line quality. Each journeyman or apprentice handled whichever task he performed best, explains Tanner:

Whenever a riflemaker had enough business to warrant his employing two or three hands . . . there was a specialization of the work. . . . One man would devote his attention to rifling barrels and fitting breech plugs; another might be particularly handy about working patchboxes and ornaments out of brass and silver and some men were more skillful than others in laying out stocks and fitting in the actions.[19]

No matter how many employees worked in his shop, the gunsmith knew that all work produced from it reflected on his reputation. Therefore, it was in his interests to keep a watchful eye on all stages of production.

If the gunsmith wished to sign his work, he would do so by scratching his name or initials on the gun barrel or patch box, a small brass box set into the stock and fitted with a hinged cover. However, many gunsmiths did not sign their finished product. Historians speculate that some gunsmiths might have preferred anonymity, especially once the American Revolution began, since creating weapons for use against British troops would have been considered treason by the British Crown. Even before the Revolution, however, the Crown tried to discourage colonists from making their own weapons, preferring that British gunsmiths get the colonists' business.

Nevertheless, some American gunsmiths risked the Crown's wrath by not only signing their weapons but serving as official gun makers for the Continental army. These included Frederick Zorger and Jacob Dickert, both of Pennsylvania. Merrill Lindsay, in his book *The Kentucky Rifle*, notes that Dickert in particular set a standard of excellence for gunsmiths throughout the colonies: "[Dickert's] gun barrels were the standard for accuracy in the Revolutionary War."[20]

AT WORK ON A GUN BARREL

Whoever the gunsmith was, the making of a gun barrel was one of the most important, and time-consuming, steps in the process. Since he did not have a drill strong enough to bore a hole in a bar of iron, the gunsmith had to create the barrel by wrapping red-hot iron around a two-foot-long iron rod known as a mandrel. The mandrel was kept unheated, while a second, thicker rod about the same length would be heated in the forge. When the iron was ready, the gunsmith took it to the anvil and folded it around the mandrel with vigorous, heavy hammer strokes. The iron, of course, was heated till it was soft enough to be pounded into a curve. The smith would continue hammering until the two sides of the iron met and joined together into a solid weld.

The average barrel of a long rifle was about four feet long, so if the smith was making one of these he would make it in two pieces. The finished product, then, would actually be two "barrels" welded end to end. Once he finished the welding on the first piece, the gunsmith drove out the mandrel with a hammer. He used the mandrel to make the second piece and then drove it out once again. The gunsmith combined both pieces into a barrel by heating and welding them together. According to Tunis, the gunsmith had a practical reason for making a barrel in two phases: "Two feet was the practical limit on [barrel making]. He couldn't get his mandrel out of a longer tube, so he made two short lengths and welded them end to end."[21]

A new gun barrel, however, rarely came away from the anvil smooth and perfect. Thus, with the welding complete and the iron cool, the smith would grind the barrel on the grindstone to smooth out any exterior imperfections. But far more important were the interior imperfections. Despite the smith's best efforts, the mandrel rarely left behind a perfect hole. The smith had to spend a good part of his time boring the hole till it was smooth and straight. He accomplished the boring with an unusual tool called a cutter. The cutter's long, narrow handle was forged from iron, but the sharp end of the cutter was made from steel, which is harder than iron and therefore useful in a tool used to cut iron.

The gunsmith turned the cutter by hand inside the barrel. This stage of the gun-making process was extremely important because if the inside of the barrel were left rough and imperfect, the finished weapon might not fire properly. Sometimes, once the boring was

complete, the smith would go ahead and assemble the rest of the gun, leaving the interior of the barrel smooth. This type of gun was known as a smoothbore musket. However, a "grooved" barrel was in greater demand than a smooth one. Although smoothbore muskets were used in the colonies, woodsmen and colonial gunsmiths considered the grooved barrel far superior. Grooves inside the gun barrel caused the bullet to spin as it traveled down the barrel. This spin added to the bullet's velocity and accuracy; in other words, it would travel farther and be more likely to hit its target. Therefore, the cutting of grooves in the barrel's interior soon became a common part of the gun-making process.

This process was called rifling, and guns made in this fashion were known as rifles. Rifling was accomplished atop a long bench. The smith clamped the barrel in place and threaded it with a steel cutter equipped with four or five sawlike teeth. This cutter was attached to a wooden rod at one end, a sliding frame at the other. The smith used the frame to slide this "toothed" cutter through the gun barrel. He used precise movements to cut the grooves, usually about eight per barrel, in a spiral.

FLINTLOCKS FROM OTHER SOURCES

The barrel was only one part of a gun, of course, and making it was not necessarily the most time-consuming or

Reenactors craft a gun barrel at an outdoor forge. Creating gun barrels was one of the most time-consuming steps in the gun-making process.

difficult step. At least as challenging was making a flintlock, or the firing mechanism for a gun. A flintlock is made up of very small components, including taut springs that had to be precisely forged so that the gun would fire properly.

Gunsmiths forged these springs out of steel, a material stronger and more durable than iron. Smiths would file steel by hand until it reached the desired shape. They then tempered the spring using the same heating-and-cooling method they employed with

❧ WHEN A ❧ GUN FIRES

The flintlock of a gun contained its firing mechanism. Flintlock components included the priming pan, which contained gunpowder; the trigger; the spring; the frizzen; and the flint, which, when struck, created the sparks that made the gunpowder ignite and sent the bullet down the barrel. This process was both brief and complicated. The gun's priming pan would hold a pinch of gunpowder under a hinged steel cover known as the frizzen. Pulling the trigger tripped a spring that caused the frizzen to flip upward just in time to meet the descending flint. This action produced a shower of sparks that in turn ignited the gunpowder and sent the bullet on its way.

iron. Without proper tempering the springs would be either too brittle or too soft to withstand long-term use.

The other components of the flintlock, such as the frizzen and hammer, were made of iron and also filed and shaped by hand. It is perhaps no wonder that, faced with such a laborious task, most gunsmiths preferred to purchase a ready-made flintlock when they could, either from abroad or from busier gun shops that developed in colonial cities. Gunsmiths who lived in remote areas, however, did not have this option.

They would have to resort to making their own flintlocks despite the fact that raw materials were scarce. Some smiths in isolated areas were known to have melted down old saw blades for metal and smelted the ore in homemade furnaces because raw iron was not available from any other source.

WORKING WITH WOOD

Once the barrel and flintlock were assembled as one, the gunsmith turned his attention to the gun stock. Gunsmiths carved stocks out of a variety of woods, including persimmon, walnut, and maple, which had been harvested from local forests. Smiths often chose maple for the stock because its tight, curly grain was considered attractive.

Though the barrel and flintlock may have been strictly utilitarian items, the stock had to be aesthetically pleasing; the gun maker knew that his customers would demand it. He accomplished some of this look by decorating the stock with striping. The smith used one of two methods to stripe wood: He would either burn on the striping with fire or apply acid or stain. According to Tanner, "A light stain might be applied to the wood before rubbing it to a fine patina [shine] with oil."[22]

If the gun maker was making a Kentucky rifle, he would also install a patch box in the gun stock. The patch box was a particularly American innovation developed for the Kentucky rifle.

A reenactor carves a gun stock out of wood. Colonial gunsmiths applied their creative talents in order to produce aesthetically pleasing gun stocks.

ᴊ **GUNS AND SILVER** ᴊ

Some gunsmiths grew so skilled with silversmithing that their work approached artistry. The silver ornamentation on some guns is so elaborate that historians have wondered if silversmiths were responsible for the work. Henry J. Kauffman, author of *The Colonial Silversmith*, says this is doubtful: "The gun is thought to have been principally the product of the gunsmith, so if any silver work is found on the gun, it is highly likely that [the gunsmith] did it." Kauffman then goes on to describe some of the more ornate weapons of the period, including those of Pennsylvania smith Frederick Zorger, who also made rifles for the colonial army. Zorger is well known for a beautifully designed pair of pistols, thought to be made between 1765 and 1780, created for a member of the Continental Congress when that body met in York, Pennsylvania. The pistol stocks are made of curly maple and mounted with silver ornaments.

FINISHING TOUCHES

As Tanner explains, "The primary goal of all these . . . gunsmiths, regardless of the community wherein they served, was [that they] produce a conveniently portable, accurate, sturdy and dependable hunting rifle—a game setter. Secondary goals might be handsome ornamentation."[23] Still, most of the gunsmith's customers, no matter where they lived, wanted their weapons to look good. The smith obliged by either inlaying an ornament on the stock or etching a pattern on the brass patch box.

Customers usually demanded silver ornaments for their guns. Sometimes smiths pried ornaments from old guns or purchased them ready-made from overseas. But historians believe that most smiths made their own. If the gunsmith was making these ornaments himself, the silver came from coins that the smith had flattened with a hand roller. Silver was a soft enough metal that in small amounts it could be shaped and chiseled without being heated. Once the flattening was complete, the smith would chisel and file out a pattern that suited the customer's taste. He would then hammer the ornament in place.

Silver gun designs varied from customer to customer, and even from region to region. For example, Pennsylvania's large Dutch population preferred to see their rifles decorated with a large silver X. This X, also known as a hex, was a Christian symbol. The Pennsylvania Dutch believed that decorating a rifle, or anything else, with a hex would keep away witches and evil spirits.

Silver flower patterns, horse's heads, birds, and stars also found their way onto American gun stocks. After the

Revolution, ornaments shaped like an eagle, America's national emblem, became very popular.

WEAPONS FROM AMERICA AND EUROPE

The Kentucky rifle was not the only weapon used in the American colonies. Gun makers along the New England coast, for instance, almost never used the rifling process when making their products. Rather, they made smoothbore muskets, the firearm of choice among coastal New Englanders.

These New Englanders preferred muskets because they tended to hunt birds and smaller animals, unlike their counterparts on the frontier, who hunted deer, panther, and other large game. Small game was best taken at close range, something for which the musket was well suited since it was most accurate at short distances.

New England craftsmen used conventional gunsmithing methods to make the musket, but unlike their rifle-making counterparts, they skipped the step where spiral grooves were cut in the barrel. Instead, these smiths focused solely on the task of making the barrel interior as smooth as possible.

A contemporary French illustration depicts two infantrymen with muskets (left), a rifleman, and an artilleryman in the Continental army.

Gun owners throughout the colonies carried imported European-made firearms as well as those made in America. These included the English Brown Bess; the French Charleville musket, which France supplied to the Continental army in large quantities during the Revolution; and the German Jaeger sporting rifle. These weapons found their way into a colonial gunsmith's shop only when they were in need of repair. Any number of things could go wrong with a firearm: For example, the flintlock springs could break or wear out and need replacement. The gunsmith could either install a new flintlock or make his own springs at the forge. Thus, even foreign weapons eventually included American-made components.

THE GUNSMITH IN SOCIETY

The gunsmith, like most of his fellow artisans, was a solidly middle-class citizen. Gun makers lived almost everywhere in the colonies, from rural areas to cities, and while a few of the busiest gun makers did become wealthy, most earned only enough to maintain a comfortable living. Nevertheless, the gunsmith came to be seen as occupying a unique place in colonial society. His was the one American-crafted product that ended up playing a direct role in freeing the country from British rule. American militiamen would carry the firearms he crafted into battle with them, relying on his skill and craftsmanship to keep them safe and help them create their country.

CHAPTER 4

THE SILVERSMITH

Like the blacksmith and gunsmith, the silversmith toiled at the forge. He worked with a metal and depended on the combination of heat and hammering to mold raw material into whatever kind of product his customer demanded. However, the silversmith was expected to create items that were more than just useful; they had to be attractive as well. Perhaps more than any other craftsman, the silversmith was also an artist.

The work of a silversmith had to be showy and beautiful. Save for a few items like spoons, cups, and thimbles, much of what a silversmith made was rarely used by the household. Rather, it would sit on a shelf, a high-profile display of the homeowner's wealth and success.

PROTECTING THEIR WEALTH

Even though most silversmiths' clientele was limited to only the wealthiest members of their community, there was still adequate demand for their services. In part this was because banks did not exist in colonial America. To protect their money, wealthy colonists had two options: They could put their coins into a strongbox kept at home and hope nobody took it, or they could have the coins turned into plate, which was the term for a set of silver items. This second option was often the preferable one. Explains Kauffman:

It was very difficult to identify one's coins if they were luckily recovered from a thief, so they were turned into identifiable objects often bearing the imprint of the maker, and sometimes the monogram or cipher of the owner.[24]

Despite these precautions, some thieves did risk apprehension by stealing

such easily identifiable items. John Marshall Phillips notes in his book *American Silver* the number of newspaper advertisements placed by victimized owners seeking to recover missing property. He quotes one such ad, placed in the *Boston-News Letter* on November 6, 1704:

[Stolen] on Saturday the 4 . . . from Mrs. Susanna Campbell, Widow in Boston, a silver tankard that holds about two wine quarts, has Sir Robert Robinson's Coat of Arms engraven on the forepart of it, wherein are three ships, and the motto in Latin. Whoever can give true intelligence of the same, so as the owner may have it again, shall be sufficiently rewarded.[25]

A colonial family displays their silver wares in a cupboard. Silver served as a status symbol for wealthy colonial families.

The wealthy colonists needed cash for transactions like anyone else, but paper money could be used for that, and the wealthy, too, were not above using barter for their everyday purchases. So the making of plate from the bulk of one's money became a well-established practice, and even a status symbol. As one wealthy colonist remarked, "I esteem it as well politic as reputable to furnish myself with a handsome cupboard of plate."[26]

Silver plate became the most coveted part of a colonist's estate. Says author Graham Hood, "Silver remained an essential part of a rich person's estate, more flexible than land, houses and retainers, and more ostentatious and also more easily identifiable."[27]

In addition to creating aesthetically pleasing pieces, the most successful silversmiths were those who cultivated good connections. When he was not involved in hard physical labor in his shop, the smith had to spend time meeting and greeting the community leaders who would, he hoped, become his clients. Unlike the blacksmith and gunsmith, therefore, a silversmith had to have attained a level of social refinement that would make him welcome in the parlors and drawing rooms of the wealthiest colonists.

Unlike other smiths, the silversmith signed his work, either with his initials or his full name. Some smiths, like Charles Oliver Bruff of New York, advertised their marks along with their services. "I design to put the stamp of my name, in full, on all my works,"[28] Bruff said in a 1767 newspaper advertisement.

The best silversmiths gained great respect and praise for their artistic abilities, and commanded high prices for their work. Some, such as Paul Revere and Joseph Richardson, became every bit as prominent as the men for whom they made their products.

The Raw Material

As the silversmith prepared to make any piece, the first step was to line up the silver itself, either from coins the client supplied or from an old silver object the client no longer needed. In any case, the silver rarely, if ever, came in the form of raw metal. Colonial America had no silver mines. The nearest such operations were far south, in Mexico and South America, and Spain did not export the silver from these mines.

Occasionally a client might ask the smith to create a work from gold. Most smiths advertised their skills in both silver and gold because doing so gave them an added air of sophistication. Still, most coinage was in silver, so requests for works of gold were much rarer than for those of silver.

The Tools of the Silversmith

The silversmith practiced a very intricate craft. And, writes Williamson, "he works with a vast assortment of odd-named and baffling tools."[29] Williamson identified the tools listed in the last will and testament of Boston silversmith John Burt: bench vises, tools for shaping spoons, beaker irons, drawing bench and tongs, salt punches, and boiling pans. Many of these tools had very specific purposes; beaker irons, for example, were used in the making of a colonial-era container called a beaker. But the most basic tools of the silversmith were very generalized. Just as a blacksmith did, he used a forge and anvil, various sized hammers, and cutting tools. However, the silversmith had to be meticulous in caring for his tools. His hammers, for example, had to be kept in perfect condition. Any flaw in the hammer head would transfer to the metal, which had to be as perfect as possible. While a small flaw might be tolerated in an iron plow or hoe, this was not the case with a silver pitcher or teapot. So to protect the hammer, the silversmith kept the head of each covered in tallow, or wax; this kept the iron from rusting or chipping.

❧ THE TALENTED PAUL REVERE ❧

Paul Revere is best known for his midnight ride to warn Samuel Adams and John Hancock that a price had been put on their heads and that the British were about to raid ammunition hideouts. But Revere was also one of the best silversmiths of his day, renowned for his taste and highly individual style. Revere was trained in the craft by his father, Frenchman Appollos De Rivoire, who changed his name to Revere after settling in America. Appollos Revere himself was trained by John Coney, one of America's early silversmiths.

Throughout the course of his life Paul Revere pursued other crafts and occupations. He engraved pictures, made false teeth and practiced dentistry, manufactured gunpowder, carved picture frames, built a printing press, made jewelry, and even shod horses. He worked as a seal maker, built ships, made copper sheathing for boats, and in 1775 engraved the plates from which the first American paper money was issued. Revere was also a leading organizer of the Sons of Liberty and took part in the Boston Tea Party. One of the most celebrated examples of colonial silver was the bowl Revere specifically made for the Sons of Liberty.

Paul Revere was one of the most talented silversmiths of colonial America.

THE SILVERSMITH AT WORK

The silversmith always worked with a large amount of silver, so rolling coins out in a flat sheet like the gunsmith did was not practical. The smith's first step was to melt the coins down. He heated them together in a crucible, or boiling pan, atop a charcoal fire in the forge.

❧ THE WEALTH ❧ OF NATIONS

The silversmith melted and shaped into plate nearly every type of gold and silver coin in circulation during the colonial period. The American colonies were truly an international place: British coins, Spanish gold "pieces of eight," and a type of Dutch currency known as dog dollars became the raw material for forged colonial plate.

During the Revolutionary War, George Washington sent sixteen Spanish silver dollars, most likely minted in Mexico, to Philadelphia silversmith Edmond Milne with specific instructions; he wanted a set of twelve "camp cups" for his personal use. Milne forged the cups and kept the leftover silver, one and three-quarter ounces, as part of his fee.

Since the silver in coins often contained impurities, the smith would have to refine the liquid silver before it cooled. He did this by combining it with saltpeter, borax, lead, or antimony. These elements would combine with the impurities but not with the silver itself. Once this chemical reaction took place, the pure silver would float to the top, allowing the smith to pour it off into an iron mold known as a skillet.

Connecticut silversmith Daniel Burnap left behind precise descriptions of his silver-making techniques and work process in his account books. One of them contains this description of how to refine silver:

> Melt the silver in a crucible in a moderate fire. As soon as the silver is melted, fling into it a plenty of fine saltpeter. Then pour the metal off almost as soon as the saltpeter is put in & the alloy will stick to the flux & the silver left pure.[30]

The next step was to combine the molten silver with a small amount of copper, which gave the metal a richer color and made it more durable and easier to work with. As the molten liquid cooled it would solidify, forming a disc that was called an ingot. The smith removed the ingot from the skillet and used his hammers to pound the ingot into thin, workable sheets of metal.

The silversmith's work routine was not considered as physically demanding as that of the blacksmith, but he still had to use a great deal of muscle, as well as precision. He had to keep his hammering constant and even so that the thickness of the silver would stay uniform. If he pounded the silver too hard on one corner, the sheet would be uneven. Thus the smith constantly measured as he went along, using calipers to judge the thickness, and kept up his hammering until the sheet was about a quarter-inch thick.

MAKING PLATE

After so much hammering the silver would become quite brittle. So, as he worked, the smith tempered the metal. To do this he would heat it over the fire until it was red-hot. He then doused it in a mixture of water and sulfuric acid. This process was called annealing, and it strengthened the metal and made it

flexible so it could be more easily shaped into a finished product.

Techniques for making items from silver varied from smith to smith, product to product, and from era to era. For example, an early smith used a process called raising to make a cup in a fairly uncomplicated fashion. He would cut a circle out of the raised sheet and hammer it down even further with a ball-headed hammer. He would then place the circle atop a round stake and hammer it until it

Silversmiths hammer ingot into workable sheets of metal. Smiths had to hammer with great precision to ensure the sheets were of uniform thickness.

took the shape of a cup. Once he achieved the shape he wanted, he smoothed the metal with a tool called a planishing hammer. The act of using this hammer was itself called planishing, which made the metal more rigid as well as smoothing it.

However, in the late eighteenth century some silversmiths began to use a more complicated, and sophisticated, way to make a cup. During the raising process they would cut separate patterns for different parts of the cup. One piece encompassed the sides of the cup, another the bottom, and the final one the handle. Once each piece was ready, the silversmith would solder them all together.

The soldering process required a controlled pattern of heating and cooling, similar to the one used to temper both iron and silver. The smith's soldering paste was four parts molten silver and one part brass. Since a smith always had stray scraps of silver in his shop, he never had to worry about having to melt down a customer's coin to make paste. Once the paste was ready he would press the parts of the cup together and apply the paste along every seam. He then held the seam directly over the fire to temper it. Once it was heated to the proper temperature, he dipped it into a sulfuric acid bath. This last step cooled the piece and removed the rough edges of the solder so that the seam would not be so noticeable.

MAKING A TEAPOT

Objects such as pitchers, tankards, and teapots were always more complicated to fabricate, and the more skilled the smith, the more likely he was to be asked to make these items. Teapots, despite their name, were also used to serve coffee or melted chocolate during the colonial era. Because of their versatility, they were a popular piece, one that consumed a good deal of time in the smith's workshop. The primary work process for making a teapot involved hammering, molds, and the use of a lathe. Writes Kauffman, "A disk of [silver] was placed on the end of a tree stump and struck with a hollowing hammer until a saucerlike contour was obtained."[31] The smith then turned the saucer upside down, put it on a stake with a round end, and hammered the sides and edges until he shaped the saucer into a teapot.

Oftentimes the pot's handle would be made of wood rather than silver, since wood did not conduct heat well. The pot's lid was made by turning silver on a lathe. According to Kauffman, "The technique used in making the spout is somewhat shrouded in mystery,"[32] but most likely it was cast in a mold. Smiths made their own molds, usually with a model made of wood. The smith would carve a wooden model of the shape he wanted and then make an impression of the model by casting two halves of a sand

A reenactor crafts a teapot. The skills of an experienced silversmith were needed to produce a teapot that was both practical and aesthetically appealing.

mold around it. He then used the sand mold to cast the piece in silver. He would cast a teapot spout in two halves, then solder them together once the metal cooled.

A less common, and much less permanent, practice was to make the model out of wax. The wax model, when baked in a sand mold, would melt and drain off, leaving the space for the silver to enter. Under this method a model could be used only once, whereas a wooden model could be used over and over.

FINISHING TOUCHES

The work schedule of the silversmith could be fast paced and exhausting, as Forbes notes as she re-creates a typical day in Paul Revere's shop:

The silversmith continually passes from his anvil, planishing stakes and hammers to the annealing [forge]. In the [apprentice's] ears would ring the dullish beat—tat tat

A reenactor applies finishing touches to his work. Silversmiths often decorated their wares to make them more attractive.

ta-tat—of . . . hammers. [The smith would] knock the cold silver blank . . . stopping every few moments to anneal once more. Slowly, a porringer [a type of metal bowl], standing cup, tray or spoon would begin to take form.[33]

But the silversmith was an artist as well as a craftsman, and he took pains to create a product that was not only sturdy but beautiful. Thus, he spent as much time finishing and decorating a piece as he did shaping it. Sometimes he "jobbed out" the decorating to other craftsmen, such as engravers, who specialized in this kind of work. More often, though, he saw to these finishing touches himself.

A smith rarely added details to please himself, however. He always followed his customers' tastes or whatever was in fashion at the time. For example, the earliest silver produced in New England was quite austere and simple, as befit Puritan society at the time. However, by the early eighteenth century, the colonies had experienced such an influx of immigrants from different backgrounds and cultures that tastes began to change. Wealthy colonists had begun to crave a fancier style of silver plate known as rococo. Rococo avoided the plain, simple lines favored by the earlier smiths and incorporated free-flowing scrolls, shells, and other designs into the silver. But by the American Revolution tastes had

changed once again, and smiths employed another, more formal style known as classic revival, which used lighter, cleaner, more elegant lines.

The smith had many techniques at hand as he worked to make his finished project attractive to the eye and satisfactory to his customer. For example, he could use a sharp tool to literally cut a design on the surface of the silver; this process was known as engraving. Or he could chase the piece, which involved chiseling a design into the silver. If the object to be chased was hollow—such as a bowl—he would first fill the container with pitch so that it would hold its shape. The Smith drew the design he wanted to make on the container's exterior and then, with a chasing hammer and an array of dull chisels and punches, carefully and painstakingly pounded the design into the metal's surface.

Another more complicated technique was the creation of a component called silver wire. The smith kept a wire-drawing bench in his shop for this purpose. He would place the sheet of silver at one end of the bench and grippers at the other. The silversmith would pinch out a strip of silver from the sheet using the grippers and draw it out by hand, in a long wire. This process required a good deal of upper-body strength and a precise eye, since the wire had to be a certain diameter and a false move or a period of inattention could result in an uneven strip of silver. Once he was finished drawing the wire, the smith would cut it in varying lengths and solder it onto the product. He could choose a simple design or an intricate one, always to the customer's liking.

Finally, the smith might attach small silver ornaments—flowers or shells, for example—to the piece via the soldering process. These ornaments were cast from molds he carved himself. The smith called on his artistic skills to make such molds, creating fine details, elegant lines, and aesthetically pleasing shapes. During this phase of the process, silversmithing was as much a mental craft as a physical one. The silversmith fell back on that indefinable quality that artists have—the ability to imagine what others cannot and put it in physical form—as he labored to finish his piece.

Once the piece was fully decorated, the smith completed the finishing process. He polished the piece with pumice, a volcanic ash, or tripoli, which was limestone ground into a powder. Finally, he would apply jeweler's rouge, a powdered red iron ore, for a finished look.

THE SILVERSMITH AS MERCHANT

Some smiths could support themselves and even grew wealthy from making silver plate, but others had to supplement their income from silver-

smithing by importing items made from gold and silver, along with other luxury items, from Europe and selling them in their shops. An advertisement in the *South Carolina Gazette* on August 27, 1763, detailed the wares of one such silver shop, owned by a man named Thomas Yon:

> Thomas Yon, at the sign of the Golden Cup in Beef Market Square, has just imported . . . a neat assortment of jewelry, an eight day cloth, and a silver mounted gun, which he will sell for ready cash on a small advance. The silversmith's business is carried on by him as usual, and continues cleaning and polishing old plate, the same as new.[34]

In addition to selling original and premade works, the cleaning and repair of existing pieces was a large part of the business for silversmiths in certain communities. This was particularly true in Williamsburg, Virginia, where as many as sixteen silversmiths worked at one time or another but where wealthy plantation owners preferred to purchase imported English silver products instead of commissioned, American-made ones. Williamsburg smiths like James Geddy obliged by importing and selling them plate and doing repair work for their customers. It was much less expensive to repair a broken cup han-

❦ MOURNING RINGS ❧

One of the silversmith's more unusual products was the mourning ring. This custom began in Europe as a way for mourners to remember a loved one. The deceased's family would have a set of rings made to be given away at the funeral. The earliest European rings had a skull design, but in seventeenth- and eighteenth-century America, the mourning ring had become a fashion statement. Wealthy individuals set aside silver for the mourning rings their loved ones would wear. They even left explicit descriptions in their wills regarding what the rings should look like.

One of the more popular choices in the colonial period was to leave behind locks of one's hair as ring material. The silversmith would encase the hair in the ring, giving the mourner a truly lasting reminder of the deceased. Silver ornaments containing a loved one's hair, whether the individual was dead or not, eventually became so popular that silversmiths began to work it into other objects. Smiths eventually advertised their ability to encase hair in such varied objects as figurines and silver flowers.

dle than to purchase an expensive new import.

Some silversmiths, however, had to go far outside their craft for extra money. Lancaster silversmith Peter Getz, for example, ran an ad in the *Pennsylvania Herald and York General Advertiser* on April 28, 1790, informing customers that he also "furnishes artificial Teeth, perfectly resembling the real, without inconvenience to the party."[35]

Paul Revere, too, advertised his dental skills during the years before the Revolutionary War. An advertisement he ran in a Boston newspaper advised that "he [Revere] has fixed some hundred of teeth and can fix them as well as any Surgeon-Dentist whoever came from London, he fixes them in such a manner that they are not only an ornament, but of real use in speaking and eating."[36]

Then there was John Inch, a Maryland silversmith who was also, apparently, a jack-of-all-trades. He advertised that he

still carries on his silversmith's and jeweler's business, buys gold and silver, and keeps tavern as formerly, and has provided himself with a good house painter and glazier lately from London who shall work for any person reasonably. He also keeps good passage-boats, and has not of his own and others, Vessels fit to carry grain, etc. to and from any part of Chesapeake Bay.[37]

THE SILVERSMITH IN THE COMMUNITY

Because he quite literally dealt with his customers' valuables, the silversmith had to develop a reputation for honesty. "[He] had to establish himself by means of personal contact, whereas most other craftsmen could merely hang out a shingle and start to work," says Williamson. "He was probably one of the first Americans to fraternize in the interests of business. He held office wherever he could, joined every club, the most affluent church, and was active in politics. After all, a fellow assemblyman might order a tea-set from him." [38]

An accurate expression of the central role the silversmith played in colonial society is this obituary of a colonial silversmith in Philadelphia:

Joseph Richardson . . . a gentleman whose private virtues, and public spirit justly claimed the friendship, esteem and confidence of his fellow citizens and others. He served for several years as a representative of this province . . . he filled several other offices of public trust with assiduity and reputation and devoted a great deal of time to settling disputes and controversies among his neighbors and others. [39]

CHAPTER 5

THE WIG MAKER

The products crafted by the silversmith were as permanent as those of the wig maker were fleeting. Most plate was meant to last a lifetime and beyond. But a wig lasted only a few seasons or until its wearer craved a different style. Still, if plate embodied a client's wealth, a wig enhanced his image. Since social standing was so important in the larger American communities, the work of the wig maker was an important part of the social fabric.

In the earliest days of the colonies, wigs were imported from England. But by 1660 skilled wig makers had arrived in America. The wig maker was a craftsman known for both the services he offered and the products he made. He made custom-fitted wigs for the important men in his community, as well as for the middle class and for anyone else who could afford them. He also barbered those customers, sometimes on a weekly basis, in return for an annual fee. He maintained the wigs he made, curling and combing them when necessary, usually making a special trip to the client's home to do so.

Wearing wigs was so fashionable that by the end of the seventeenth century it was the practice throughout the colonies. Boys would be outfitted with wigs as early as age seven. Everyone from blacksmiths and innkeepers to plantation owners and clergymen (and some women) wore a wig when the occasion required—if they could afford to do so. They wore them to church, to their place of business, to court, or on any number of social occasions.

The colonial wig maker almost always worked in a town or city, since that was where those who had the money to pay for wigs usually lived. Wigs were very expensive. For the price of one wig, a colonist could purchase an entire suit of clothes, historians say. However, most colonists felt the expense was worth it because a wig enhanced one's social status. Although some wig makers catered to women, the demand was largely for men's wigs. Men were the leaders in their communities, so they were the ones most concerned with their image. The well-dressed colonial man always wore a wig. And even though the wig maker, being a craftsman, did not enjoy the same social status as many of his clients, his shop did become a gathering place for the most important men in the community.

The wig maker's work was not as physically demanding as that of the gunsmith, blacksmith, or silversmith. Instead, wig making required fine-motor skills such as weaving and sewing. In addition, the wig maker often dealt one-on-one with his clientele, long after the customer took the wig home. Therefore, his social skills had to be superb.

THE WIG MAKER'S SHOP

The wig maker oversaw a large staff in a small workshop. He usually employed at least three or four apprentices and journeymen, sometimes more, to serve customers who were barbered regularly at his shop. Wig making was a team effort, more so than most crafts, so the craftsman did his best to obtain the best employees he could—even to

the point of enticing them away from the competition, as one Williamsburg wig maker alleged in a 1745 advertisement in the *Virginia Gazette.* The wig maker, Andrew Anderson, accused his competitor across the street, Alexander Finnie, of luring away one of his journeymen in an unethical fashion, as noted by a pamphlet on wig making published by the Colonial Williamsburg Foundation:

> Whereas my honest neighbor, that has advertis'd for Two or Three Journeyman, has lately seduced One from My Service, in a clandestine and undermining manner; which I am well persuaded, that no man but for One of his principles would have done.[40]

Wig makers like Finnie probably lured each other's prize employees with the promise of higher wages, since working conditions hardly varied from shop to shop. Wig shops were crowded, noisy, and sometimes frantic places. Plans for a wig shop in Williamsburg depicted a single room sixteen by twenty feet, which was expected to accommodate the master wig maker, his helpers and customers, and a myriad of tools.

Despite these cramped conditions, the wig shop was a convivial place, thanks to the social skills that the wig maker, as well as his staff, took care to cultivate. He would entertain his

A colonial wig maker powders a wig outside his shop. Colonial Americans of all ages wore wigs to enhance their social standing.

The wig maker's shop was a lively place. Wig makers entertained their customers with gossip or news while they were fitted for a wig or got a shave.

customers with news and gossip while they underwent measurements for wigs, waited while a new wig was powdered, or got a shave. Customers endured the overcrowded shop for the pampering, including perfumes and powdering, they received and for a chance to gossip with other important clients visiting at the same time.

THE WIG MAKER'S TOOLS

One of the wig maker's more important tools was the wig block. A wig block had two components: a leather container shaped like a human head and a wooden base to hold it. The block was hollow and had a door to keep his tools inside. But the block's most prominent function was to hold the wig as the maker added its finishing touches. The shop also had a weaving bench, where the wig maker wove hair. A colonial wig was made of woven rows of hair of varying lengths. Last but not least were the wig maker's barbering tools: a straight razor, soap, soap containers, and a bowl for hot water.

RAW MATERIALS

The wig maker purchased hair from colonial hair merchants, who either imported it or obtained it locally. White, black, brown, and gray hair were the most prized, but almost any color hair would do. Such merchants would advertise for hair, as evidenced by this colonial newspaper advertisement placed by a Williamsburg hair merchant named George Long:

> The subscriber proposes purchasing Hair for Wigs and hopes he will soon be able to supply wigmakers with that article, of different kinds. He is in want of a quantity of human hair . . . of any colour, for which he will give one shilling per ounce.[41]

The client would select the color, though not the actual hair, for his wig. The wig maker himself ultimately chose the hair for each wig he made.

TAKING MEASUREMENTS

The process of making the wig began with the customer—or, rather, with the removal of the customer's hair. An apprentice or journeyman, or perhaps the wig maker himself if the client was an important-enough person, used a straight razor to shave the man's head until he was completely bald. Wig wearers, men and women, went bald for several reasons. The wig would not fit comfortably if the client still had his hair, and in order to make proper measurements the wig maker had to deal with a bald pate. Moreover, according to historians, it was so difficult for the client to keep his natural hair clean that if he was going to wear a wig he might as well go hairless.

The wig maker began his work by measuring the customer's head. To do so, he gathered five long strips of paper, each about an inch wide, and used them as a kind of measuring tape. First, the wig maker would lay a strip from the top center of the forehead over the head to the nape of the neck. Using his scissors he would cut slits in the paper to mark where the center of the forehead began and where the nape ended.

He would repeat the process, taking care to measure as accurately as possible. He measured the length between the left and right temple, circling the paper strip around the back of the head. He measured the head from ear to ear, over the top of the head; from the middle of either cheek around the back of the head; and from the top center of the forehead to either temple. The wig maker drew on his years of experience to form a pattern of the customer's head, laying out each strip of paper and assembling them according to the cuts he had made.

PREPARING THE HAIR

The wig maker delegated the hair preparation to his apprentices and journeymen. The apprentice sorted hair by color. He would tie each color in bundles and dust the bundles with sand to soak up any excess hair oil. Then it was time to shake out the sand and comb each bundle until the hair

❧ PULLING ❧ TEETH

The wig maker also served as a dentist in his community, pulling rotting or aching teeth. Many wig makers advertised this fact along with their wig-making services, says John Woodforde in his book *The Strange Story of False Hair.* Woodforde cites this advertisement, published in New York in 1768 by wig maker James Daniel: "James Daniel, wigmaker and hairdresser also operates on the teeth, a business so necessary in this city."

The actual tooth-pulling was a painful procedure for the patient, since colonial wig makers had no anesthetic. Most patients prepared for the procedure by getting drunk at the local tavern, thereby numbing themselves somewhat to the pain, and then enlisting friends to help them into the wig maker's shop. The wig maker extracted the tooth with a slightly curved rod that had a little hinged claw. He would insert the rod in the patient's mouth, firmly grip the tooth with the claw, then yank it out.

lay smooth. The apprentice used a special wig maker's comb called a hackle, which actually looked more like a brush: It had a flat back and several rows of fine teeth that easily unsnarled tangled hair.

The wig maker took over from there. He put each hair bundle into a vise. The wig maker's vise was a kind of clamping system that was permanently fixed to a tabletop in a horizontal position. One end of the bundle of hair was clamped into the vise while the craftsman rolled the remainder of the bundle onto a clay curling pin, since most wigs of that era were curly. Curling the hair at this stage helped hold its shape later in the process. After every bundle was curled, the wig maker handed the job over to a journeyman. The journeyman boiled the curls in water for about three hours, observing the pot carefully so that it maintained a steady boil. He then dried the bundles by placing them in a hot oven. Again, he watched the process carefully to make sure the hair would not burn.

Some, though apparently not all, wig makers added an extra step by putting the hair through a second round of baking. The curls were laid in a pile and covered in a shell of bread dough, which the craftsman likely obtained from a local baker. The curls and dough were baked in the wig maker's oven until the bread was done. This procedure allowed the hair to absorb extra moisture from the dough, giving it life and body for when the wig maker moved on to the next stage. When the bread was fully baked, the curls were broken out of the bread loaf. They were then placed in the oven for a final, brief baking.

Once the baking process was complete, the hair was put aside to cool. The wig maker and his helpers removed the cooled hair from the clay pins and combed it with hackles. It was at this point that the wig maker would inspect his raw materials one last time. If the customer preferred a mottled wig, as was sometimes the fashion, the craftsman would take apart a few curls and mix the hair colors.

WEAVING THE WIG
The wig maker used his practiced eye to decide how long or short each row of hair should be, using the pattern he had made earlier as his guide. To weave a row, which was called a welt in wig-maker parlance, the wig maker employed his weaving bench. Of all his tasks, hair weaving was probably the most time-consuming and laborious. A weaving bench contained two upright posts that could hold three to six silk threads, each the basis of a welt, between them. The wig maker stretched the threads in place and wove hair upon them. His style of weaving varied according to the type of wig he wanted to make. For example, a wig that incorporated many curls required a much different weave than a wig with a smoother style.

The wig maker wove one welt at a time, using a few strands of hair at a time, until the welt was as long and wide as the wig and pattern called for. Once the first welt was complete, the wig maker would wind it around one of the posts to get it out of his way. Then he would begin another. After all the welts were completed, it was time to make the wig's headpiece.

CREATING A HEADPIECE
The actual making of the headpiece was delegated to a journeyman. This helper would use the skull pattern the wig maker had created earlier. He would lay a piece of tightly woven cotton or silk netting atop it and cut out a piece that matched the pattern.

He would then drape the cutout piece over the wig block and sew an inch-wide ribbon of silk around its edges; this added feature helped the wig hold its shape. Since even the finest wig was often uncomfortable to wear, and came off at the most inopportune times, the journeyman frequently added a drawstring or strap and buckle at the back of the wig so that the wearer could draw the fit tighter if he wished.

When the skullcap was complete, the wig maker brought in the welts and finished the wig himself. With the skullcap still atop the wig block, the craftsman lay the long and short welts

Wig crafting involved a very complex process. In this French illustration, wig makers and journeymen work on wigs in various stages of completion.

parallel on top of it, beginning at the back of the head and working upward and forward. He sewed the welts in place, one at a time, using a straight, simple stitch.

FINISHING TOUCHES

The wig was not complete until the customer returned to the shop for a final fitting. At the fitting, the wig maker would place the wig atop the client's head. He would trim it if the hair was uneven and recurl the hair if it looked limp in places, using a comb, curling iron, and his fingers.

The finishing touch was always the powdering. Fashion dictated that wigs be worn powdered. The wig maker's customer had his choice of a variety of colors: white, gray, or even black. This suggests that powder substituted for hair dye in the wig maker's shop. When the powdering was ready to begin, an apprentice handed the client a paper cone, or mask, to protect his eyes and face, as well as a jacket to protect his clothing. The wig maker used a bellows to blow the powder on the wig. He also applied perfume if the customer wished, and many did.

Simple wigs cost upward of forty-three shillings—enough money to purchase a man's shirt, pants, and shoes in colonial America. Wig prices varied a great deal, but for the most part, the more formal the wig, the higher the purchase price.

CARING FOR THE WIG

Such an expensive purchase required regular maintenance: fresh powder, fresh perfume. The wig maker usually provided this maintenance in person, traveling from house to house himself. Some southern plantation owners even reserved a special room in their large homes for the services of the wig maker. These areas were known as "powdering rooms."

If a special dinner or political gathering had been planned in town, however, the wig maker would not have the time to go to every single one of his customers and "freshen" their wigs. So, instead, he sent his apprentices from house to house to fetch the wigs and bring them into the shop. After the wigs were combed, powdered, and perfumed for the special event, the apprentices would return them to their owners. Wigs usually made these journeys inside a special wig box, which contained a head-shaped piece or block upon which the wig rested.

BARBERING AND DOCTORING

A customer paid the wig maker a modern equivalent of four hundred dollars a year to keep his wig looking good. This fee—on top of the initial purchase price—made the wig a substantial investment in colonial society. The fee usually included barbering service as well. It was the fashion for colonial men to go clean shaven; only woodsmen would dare go about wearing a beard. And only the poorest of men shaved themselves at home. Even a man who did not wear a wig often paid a wig maker an annual fee, about two pounds (roughly two hundred dollars today) a year, to shave him weekly. The notable exception might be a wealthy landowner, who would acquire a trained slave or servant to shave him at home.

The colonial barber—either a journeyman, apprentice, or the master wig maker himself—used a straight razor, a long-handled instrument with a single, sharp blade, to shave his client. He would soap the customer's face with a thick lather and then shave off the whiskers with careful, even strokes. While the customer had his shave, one of the store's employees might be refreshing his wig for him, applying fresh powder and perfume.

The wig maker/barber performed a whole host of services that had little to do with hair or barbering. He provided basic medical services in his shop, pulling sore teeth, treating black eyes with leeches so the swelling would go down, and performing bloodletting, a procedure believed to cure illness or reduce fever. The patient clutched a wooden staff while he was bled in order to better open up the vein. His arm was then wrapped in a cloth bandage to stop the bleeding. This process was later immortalized

A wig maker powders a client's wig. Wig makers routinely visited their clients in order to powder and perfume their wigs.

in the red-and-white barber's pole—red for the blood, white for the bandage—that is still in use today.

WIG STYLES

The wig maker produced literally dozens of wig styles that fell in and out of fashion as the years passed. Some of the more popular styles included the great wig. This type of wig involved a high head of hair and cascading curls. Wealthy gentlemen favored the great wig, which was quite formal and expensive, but tradesmen, merchants, and other working men preferred a more practical style, like the Ramillies or Tye wigs. A great wig was likely to get in the way of a physical activity and would have had to have been pinned up before such activity commenced.

The Ramillies—less expensive than the great wig—was a smooth-topped wig with a braid in back. The Tye was similar except that its tail was unbraided and much shorter, like a pigtail. Wearers of the Ramillies or Tye usually adorned them with a black or

❧ THE FINE ART OF BLOODLETTING ❧

Bloodletting was practiced for well over a thousand years before it was performed in the wig and barber shops of colonial America. Bloodletting was based on the idea that the body had four humours, or liquids—blood, phlegm, yellow bile, and black bile—and these humours had to be in balance to maintain good health. The letting of blood was one of the techniques used to restore health; patients might also be forced to vomit or fast, although only bloodletting was performed in the wig maker's shop.

The tools of bloodletting were as ancient as the practice itself. In addition to the staff the patient clenched in his fist, the practitioner performing the bloodletting used a lancet, or blade, to open up a vein. The blood would be caught in a shallow bowl held by an assistant. One to four pints was usually the limit of what could be drawn.

Colonial wig makers used lancets, or blades, to perform the ancient practice of bloodletting.

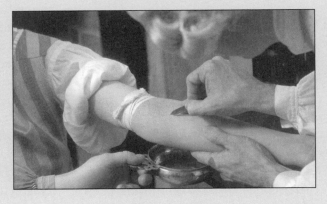

brightly striped ribbon. The bob wig was one style that combined the formal and the practical, since it had no tail but did sport a set of tight curls at either side.

WIG MAKERS FOR WOMEN

The demand for wigs primarily came from men, but larger cities, like Philadelphia and Boston, did provide enough business for wig makers who catered to women. Even wig makers who specialized in male wigs sometimes made hairpieces for the wives and daughters of their customers. Up until the middle of the eighteenth century, women rich and poor wore their own hair. Later, fashionable hairstyles became so complicated that they were impossible to care for at home. Women who could afford it thus resorted to custom-made wigs, which would be combed and cared for by someone else. And like their male counterparts, women who wore wigs went bald for the privilege of doing so.

THE WIG MAKER'S PLACE IN SOCIETY

Like most craftsmen, the wig maker did not grow rich from his craft. But he did provide what a well-dressed man needed to get along in society, and thus enjoyed a good reputation. And like the silversmith, the wig maker had many important friends. Nonetheless, most wig makers pursued side occupations in order to earn a living. More often than not, a wig maker would sell inexpensive, ready-made wigs and hairpieces that were imported from Europe and sold on a first-come, first-serve basis either right aboard the ship when it docked or in the wig maker's shop.

Poor colonists who wanted to look fashionable tied a queue, a long, narrow hairpiece that resembled a pigtail, to the back of their natural hair with a string or bought a ready-to-wear wig. These cheap wigs were often ill fitting and were never made of human hair. Usually the hair was taken from horses, goats, and cows. Cheap wigs might be made out of copper wire or even feathers. Wealthy colonists and anyone else who could afford it, however, paid the wig maker a higher price for a custom-made wig.

Some wig makers sold merchant goods along with the wigs they made. For example, during the 1770s, wig maker Edward Charlton of Williamsburg recorded in his ledgers the sale of "butter . . . eight pounds of chocolate, five hundred limes, stockings, a piece of linen and . . . beer."[42] Charlton also partnered with a local bookkeeper to purchase and operate the local theater. Still other wig makers kept inns and taverns and served on the Williamsburg Common Council.

THE END OF AN ERA

The wig maker's craft was a fleeting one, since his product began to go out of fash-

❧ WIGS IN THE PULPIT ❧

Wigs were not very popular among one segment of society: the clergy. As Bill Severn describes in his book *The Long and Short of It: Five Thousand Years of Fun and Fury over Hair*, Boston minister Increase Mather railed against the wearing of wigs. He warned his congregation that wigs were "Horrid Bushes of Vanity . . . contrary to the Light of Nature and to express scripture." Severn also says that missionary John Eliot blamed wigs for the 1675 Indian uprising known as King Philip's War. God had used the uprising to punish colonists, Eliot said, because "they disfigure themselves with hair that is none of their own . . . an abomination unseemlie in the sight of God."

Samuel Sewall, judge of the Salem witchcraft trials, made the abolishment of wigs his personal crusade. But even the clergy's misgivings fell away as prominent ministers like Cotton Mather, Increase's son, began to wear them. Soon, clergymen who railed about wigs from the pulpit were wearing them as they preached.

Despite the clergy's condemnation of wigs, prominent ministers like Cotton Mather (pictured) continued to wear them.

ion by the mid–eighteenth century. "In general, wigs grew smaller as the eighteenth century aged," Tunis writes. "They began to disappear not too long after the Revolution, though some elderly men clung to them into the 1800s. Better the old wig than a bald pate."[43]

Nevertheless, during their heyday, wig makers were an important thread in the fabric of colonial life. They serviced America's most wealthy and prominent men, who also used their shops as gathering places where they could discuss the important issues of the day.

CHAPTER 6

THE PRINTER

Printers were craftsmen who catered to the intellect. Their products probably touched more lives than those made by other craftsmen. The books, newspapers, and other materials they printed nurtured a new American culture that gradually emerged from the shadow cast by British rule. Printers published the thoughts and opinions of America's first great thinkers, as well as practical information colonists could use in their daily lives.

"THE PRESERVER OF ALL ARTS"

Boston printer Isaiah Thomas, reflecting on his profession near the end of his life, called printing "that art which is the preserver of all arts." Printing, he added, "is worthy of the attention of the learned and the curious."[44] Many of Thomas's colleagues were not as literate as he, but surely most understood the unique opportunity their craft afforded them: to have an impact on society. Thus, most printers took their high-profile community role seriously. Many a printer, though not well schooled himself, had the courage to publish articles that criticized the British Crown. Those printers who could read and write invariably used their craft to express their own views, even to the point of endangering their lives and livelihoods. Thomas himself barely escaped imprisonment due to the antiroyalist stance of his newspaper, the *Massachusetts Spy*. In 1721 James Franklin announced in his newspaper, the *News-Courant*, that his policy would be "to Expose the Vices and Follies of Persons of all Ranks and Degrees under feign'd names and this the Publisher is resolv'd to persue without Fear, or Affection, to any man."[45] This policy eventually cost Franklin his freedom; he was imprisoned for printing seditious works, some of which had been penned by his younger brother Benjamin. But the experience did not sour the elder Franklin on his craft. After he was released from prison he left Boston for Rhode Island, where he established that colony's first newspaper.

The printer may have fed the colonies' intellectual life, but he was also a businessman: Like other craftsmen, the printer wanted first and foremost to make money. And in spite of the fact that many of his fellow colonists were illiterate or, at the very least, ill schooled, the colonial printer found a huge appetite for his product. The first book printed on American soil rolled off the presses as early as 1640. Less than sixty years later, newspapers had sprung up everywhere in the colonies, despite the Crown's best efforts to suppress them.

Benjamin Franklin greets visitors to his printing press. Franklin used his press to publish many of his writings.

A PHYSICAL ACT

Even though the printer made a unique product, he still had a good deal in common with his fellow craftsmen the blacksmith, the silversmith, the gunsmith, and even the wig maker. For one thing, the act of printing was very physical. Operating a printing press by hand was heavy, difficult, and time-consuming work, even when a printer had plenty of help. Printing a book, newspaper, or legal proclamation could be a painstakingly slow process, like the work of the gunsmith and wig maker, because every piece of type had to be put in place by hand.

❧ BENJAMIN FRANKLIN: ❧ STATESMAN AND PRINTER

Benjamin Franklin was undoubtedly one of the most creative men ever born in America. He was a diplomat, inventor, scientist, statesman, signer of the Declaration of Independence, philosopher, and author, but he began as a printer. And, as with most things, he pursued that craft in a superb fashion.

Franklin began as an apprentice to his brother James. He learned the printing trade while pursuing his education. He read Plutarch, Daniel Dafoe, John Bunyan, and Cotton Mather while he was still a boy. He began writing articles for the paper when he was fifteen. His controversial views led to his brother being imprisoned for a month, and though James eventually began printing again, he and Benjamin had a falling out and Benjamin made his way to Philadelphia and finally London, where he worked for several printers. He returned to Philadelphia in 1726, and three years later he bought the *Pennsylvania Gazette*, a rather dull weekly he transformed with his witty writing style.

Four years later, in 1733, he published *Poor Richard's Almanack* under the pen name Richard Saunders. This little book became the most popular product he ever produced; historians believe that *Poor Richard's* strongly influenced American society. But in 1736 Franklin began to pursue other occupations. He became clerk of the Pennsylvania General Assembly that year and was appointed deputy postmaster of Philadelphia the following year. He founded the American Philosophical Society in 1743. Finally, in 1748 Franklin sold his printing business. One year later he wrote a set of proposals that led to the establishment of the Academy of Philadelphia, which later became the University of Pennsylvania. In 1750 he was elected to the Pennsylvania Assembly.

Like the silversmith and wig maker, the printer relied on his contacts with the important men of the community. And like the gunsmith and blacksmith, the printer's customer base was highly democratic. Anyone who had a few pence or shillings could purchase one of his books, newspapers, or almanacs. The information and entertainment he provided was eagerly consumed by anyone who could read.

The printer's craft, however, was really a team effort. A blacksmith, gunsmith, or silversmith could conceivably work alone in a small shop that did not see a lot of business. A printer, on the other hand, needed at least two pressmen—and usually more—to run his printing press while he oversaw a myriad of other details.

The printer and his crew of journeymen and apprentices cranked out pages upon pages of product over the course of a twelve-hour day. They worked as a team in a noisy, crowded environment; the printer worked out front, selling the books he had printed and bound, while his helpers delivered newspapers or magazines. Usually he relied on others, local writers who brought their handwritten materials to the shop, to provide his material, or he reprinted material that had originally appeared in European newspapers. He also took care to include stories that entertained as well as informed. Almanacs, which colonial farmers depended on for weather predictions, included such fillers as jingles, jokes, and home remedies.

For the most part, the printer was an urban craftsman. So much of his craft dealt with the everyday business of a large city or town—the printing of new laws; travel schedules for freight wagons, ferries, and stagecoaches; even the sermons of popular clergymen—that he found it worth his while to settle in a heavily populated area.

PAPER AND INK

But before he could begin the printing process, a printer had to acquire raw material. His raw material was paper and ink, and the American printer relied on imported products from Europe, at least at the beginning. Tunis explains: "American printers had special American burdens. Paper was hard to get. Most of it came from abroad and when a ship was late, the press waited."[46] However, colonial paper mills were open and operating in most communities by the end of the seventeenth century.

As for printer's ink, it was made of lampblack, or soot, and linseed oil boiled with rosin. Most printers imported their ink from England, but a few of the more enterprising ones, like Benjamin Franklin and Christopher Sower of Germantown, made their own ink and sometimes sold it to their colleagues. Ink would not be manufactured in quantity in America until after the war, however, when Justus Fox, also of Germantown, began to sell ink by the keg and pot to other printers in the middle colonies.

TOOLS OF THE TRADE

The tools of the printer ranged from tiny to large and unwieldy. The printing press itself was made of wood and metal and bolted to the floor in the printer's shop; it was also braced at the shop's ceiling. The main frame of the press was rectangular in shape, with a lever at the top that the printer used to pull down a thick wooden block, known as a platen, against a sheet of paper to press the paper against the inked type. The press also contained a long, flat tray on which the paper and type were positioned.

Presses were incredibly expensive to purchase. Adding to that expense was the cost of shipping them from Europe. The printer spent anywhere from 75 to 100 pounds (roughly $7,000 to $10,000 today) to set up a one-press shop, and the largest shops had three presses or more.

Printers' type proved as much of an expense as the press itself. Type— letters of the alphabet and punctuation—was cast from a mold out of a molten mixture of lead and antimony. "[Printers] imported type at high prices. A printer's stock type was often worth more than all else he owned,"[47] writes Tunis. Foundries dedicated to the casting of printers' type were established in America by the end of the eighteenth century, but through most of the colonial era, type had to be imported.

THE COMPOSING PROCESS

The printing of any page, whether for a newspaper, book, proclamation, or almanac, followed a well-ordered process that was repeated many times during the course of a day. It began when the compositor, usually a journeyman, assembled the page by hand, letter by letter.

He worked atop a composing case, which held the type. Since the pages were pressed directly onto the type, the compositor would compose his sentences from right to left so that the actual printed page could be read left to right. He would pick out letters and set them in the composing stick, a small, three-sided tray he could lengthen or shorten depending on how long the line of printed words was to be. Once the stick was full he would drop it into a page-sized tray called a galley. A full galley was equal to a printed page. Once a galley was filled, another helper, often an apprentice, would take over temporarily.

This apprentice inked the galley with an ink ball, a leather-covered ball stuffed with hair and padded with wool. Once the galley was inked either he or the compositor made a copy of the galley, known as a proof, by laying a piece of paper on top of it and pounding the paper with a rawhide

A printer arranges type to create a printed page. In colonial America, type was made of a mixture of lead and antimony and cast from a mold.

mallet. He gave the proof to the master printer, who noted any errors. The compositor then corrected the errors by removing any errant letters or punctuation, reinked the page, and made more proofs. This process continued until the printer was satisfied.

Once a galley was finished, it went to a journeyman called the stoneman. The stoneman worked on a level surface called an imposing stone and assembled two or more galleys side by side, depending on the final product. He framed the pages with an iron form called a chase and inserted wooden blocks, known as furniture, in the empty spaces around and between the pages. The final step involved hammering wedges between the chase itself and the furniture. This ensured that the pages would be locked in place and not fall apart when they were picked up and put on the press.

THE PRINTING PROCESS

Two journeymen printers worked as a team at the press. Their working day was disciplined and well organized; a pair of skilled journeymen could theoretically turn out twenty-four hundred printed sheets in the course of a ten-hour day. However, the pressmen's output depended on speed, luck, and a lack of mistakes during the course of the day, and of course these variables changed with shop conditions, sometimes daily.

The two pressmen, known as First and Second as they worked, knew their roles and rigidly adhered to their duties. Second would prepare the ink by spreading it over a stone slab with what resembled a putty knife, a process that surely left him with ink-stained hands and clothes by the end of the day. He would dip two ink balls in the ink and "beat" the type, which was then slid in place beneath the platen.

First, who was also known as the puller, spent his time getting the paper ready: He would stretch a damp sheet of paper on top of a device known as a tympan, which was a light flame hold-

Reenactors work at a printing press. Skilled printers could turn out four hundred printed sheets during a ten-hour workday.

ing the paper in place. He would then paste small pieces of cardboard to the tympan so that the paper would be in exactly the right position. Finally, he would lower a device known as a frisket over the paper. The frisket was composed of a single sheet of paper surrounded by a light wooden frame. Holes cut in the frisket made certain that the printing paper only received the type impression; thus it protected the paper from stray ink spots.

With the tympan, paper, frisket, and inked type now ready and in place, First grabbed the press handle and pulled it toward him. The handle pulled the platen downward against the tympan and paper, squeezing the paper against the type. Platens were heavy and delivered a lot of squeeze. It took a lot of effort to move them, and plenty of pressmen must have been left with aching shoulders at the end of the day after pulling the platen handle a thousand or more times.

Once the page was printed, First would pull the finished product out of the press. Second perused it a final time before putting it in the "heap," a pile of finished pages.

MAKING A BOOK

If the finished pages were to be made into a book, that book would have to be folded, gathered, and bound. Sometimes the printer jobbed out the binding to another craftsman who specialized in book binding. But more

often the job was handled in-house, by the printer and his employees. The making of a book was even more complex than the printing. It involved twenty-eight steps, including folding, pressing, sewing, and trimming the pages.

The process began by laying groups of printed pages, called signatures, atop each other on a sewing frame. The craftsman stitched cords, with linen thread, to the back folds of the pages; the cords formed horizontal ridges across the spine, the mark of a finely bound book. He then covered the book, either with thin leather (sheepskin or calfskin) or a combination of leather and decorated paper. Says Williamson, "The (leather) case is fitted around the book and secured by additional sewing, or, in a less sturdy book, by pasting the end sheets of the first and last sections to the board of the cover."[48]

The printer decorated his new book with the help of stamps, or dies. The dies were engraved with a specific design, heated, and applied to the leather. The first book printed in America was religious in nature: *The Whole Booke of Psalmes.* Printers also bound schoolbooks, legal and medical handbooks, and pamphlets called "ready reckoners," which gave the values of coins from colony to colony.

But the most popular bound book had no printing in it at all; it was, in fact, blank. Plantation owners and farmers used blank books for crop records, craftsmen used them for business purposes, courthouses and churches for record keeping. Any good printer made sure he had a number of blank books on hand in his shop.

THE AMERICAN ALMANAC

Almanacs were among the most popular items the colonial printer produced. Almanacs were pamphlets that compiled statistics, scientific information, entertainment, and homilies on virtue and good behavior. American printers were publishing them as early as the mid–seventeenth century. William Bradford of New York used his 1686 almanac, *America's Messenger*, to introduce himself and his printing business to his readers: "Hereby understand that after great Charge and Trouble, I have brought great Art and Mystery of Printing [to] this part of America," Bradford wrote in an advertisement for *America's Messenger.* "[I believe] it may be of great service to you in several respects, hoping to find Encouragement, not only in this Almanack, but what else I shall enter upon for the use and service of the Inhabitants of these Parts." [49]

Almanacs published by Bradford and other printers contained information on phases of the moon, sun, and tides; weather predictions; planting times; schedules of coaches and boats; court dates; and even snakebite cures. All of this information was much appreciated by people who planted crops and lived by the sea. Some of this material the printer obtained from government sources. As for the rest of the material, "the printer tried to associate himself with some person skilled in mathematics who should be able to compile annually an almanac for the local meridian," [50] says Lawrence C. Wroth in his book *The Colonial Printer.*

While Benjamin Franklin's *Poor Richard's Almanack* attained lasting fame, printers from all over the colonies published such volumes on a regular basis, and readers devoured them. Says Wroth of the American almanac, "The familiar handbook of every member of the household, pored over in the winter evenings by father and sons, mother and daughters, these little books of utility take on in view of this feature of their content greater importance among American writings than they have been formerly credited with." [51]

THE AMERICAN NEWSPAPER

Most colonial printers aspired to publish a newspaper, since these offered the best chance of making money. About half of an average colonial newspaper was devoted to paid advertising, and that, combined with payments from the paper's list of regular subscribers, meant a steady income for the printer.

❧ THE JOHN PETER ZENGER STORY ❧

John Peter Zenger served his apprenticeship with the prominent New York printer William Bradford. He founded his own newspaper, *New York Weekly Journal*, in 1733 and went head-to-head against his former master. Bradford's paper supported the royal governor while Zenger's paper promoted the Popular Party of New York, a group of antiroyalists. Zenger's *Weekly Journal* attacked the royal governor and his supporters, an act that landed him in jail.

A grand jury empaneled in 1734 heard charges of sedition against Zenger and the *Weekly Journal*. However, the grand jury refused to return any indictments. Governor William Cosby obtained a warrant for Zenger's arrest in November anyway, jailing him for nine months. Zenger continued to edit his paper from his jail cell, and on August 4, 1775, his case came to trial.

Well-known lawyer Andrew Hamilton agreed to defend him against libel charges. Then, as Frank Luther Mott records in *American Journalism*, Hamilton made a stirring speech on press freedom in court:

> The question before the court and you gentlemen of the jury is not of small nor private concern; it is not the cause of the poor printer, nor of New York, alone. . . . It may . . . affect every freeman that lives under a British government on the main of America. It is the best cause. It is the cause of liberty.

The jury acquitted Zenger, who immediately went home to run his printing business.

A painting depicts the trial of printer John Peter Zenger in 1734.

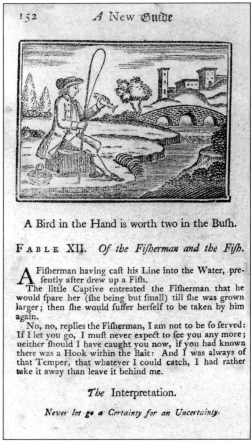

Pictured is a page from the 1732 edition of Franklin's Poor Richard's Almanack.

Most colonial newspapers were published weekly, usually in or around a large commercial center like New York or Philadelphia. In 1735 five newspapers circulated in Boston alone, even though at the time the city itself had fewer than twenty thousand residents.

Printers usually relied on local writers to bring the news to them. Yet despite the fact that newspapers were a business venture, many colonial printers had to be careful what they printed; including an article for its sensational value was not allowed. Thomas, who had firsthand experience running a newspaper before and during the Revolutionary War, later wrote of his experience with British censorship. "The fathers of Massachusetts kept a watchful eye on the press," Thomas is recorded as saying, "and in neither a religious nor civil point of view were they disposed to give it much liberty. But the civil and ecclesiastical rulers were fearful that if it was not under wholesome restraints, contentions and heresies would arise among the people."[52]

The British Crown had appointed licensors of the press, who were required by law to review all materials before they appeared in the newspapers. If the printer refused to submit his articles, he risked imprisonment; the royal governor could also decide to seize his printing press and other assets.

THE PRINTER'S BREAD AND BUTTER

Printers had a financial incentive to toe the line where the British were concerned, since their bread and butter was the printing of laws and official proclamations issued by the government. Writes Wroth,

> [Printers] . . . put out in type the many instruments—proclamations and the like—formerly

copied with much labor by scribes not necessarily either skillful, accurate or reliable, and afterwards published by the county sheriffs through the ancient and limited method of proclamation by word of mouth.[53]

The government provided a tremendous amount of material, including new laws and official business, and some printers openly curried the Crown's favor in return for a contract to publicize such material. Bradford, who became the first printer to produce a set of votes and proceedings for a colonial assembly, was a strong supporter of the royalists and often published their points of view in his newspaper. Other printers, however, maintained a delicate balance throughout the colonial period by publishing both antiroyalist material and government documents.

❧ WOMEN PRINTERS ☙

Women were generally barred from the crafts unless they were practicing them in their own homes. Almost none practiced a craft on a professional basis, but the one exception appeared to be printing. A number of colonial women ran printing businesses after their husbands died. The earliest such woman to do so was Diana Nuthead of Maryland, widow of William. She succeeded her husband in 1694, signing a bond to take over the shop with an X, meaning that this new businesswoman could not read or write.

Printers' widows had an advantage over the wives of other craftsmen in that a printer had a trained team in place to run the press and perform strenuous, physical duties. Moreover, early printing shops were usually part of the household and the printer's wife often worked in the front with customers, selling books or other printed items.

Usually printers' widows ran the business until they remarried or one of their sons took over. There were exceptions, however. Anne Franklin, widow of James, ran her late husband's print shop for twenty-eight years, getting help not from sons but from her two daughters.

When Mary Katherine Goddard's brother had to abandon his printing business temporarily, she took over the business for him, producing a newspaper, almanacs, and other printed materials. She stepped aside for him when he returned in 1784 but did not leave the business world. She later became Baltimore's postmistress and ran a bookstore.

Bostonians make a bonfire of stamped documents in protest of the 1765 Stamp Act. The act required all printed materials to carry a tax stamp.

THE PRINTER AS BUSINESSMAN

Even the most successful printer was chronically short of cash, since advertisers and subscribers were often slow to pay their bills. It was up to the printer to collect these debts, and a few did so quite publicly, as Frank Luther Mott detailed in his book *American Journalism.* Printer John Peter Zenger, for example, ran this advertisement in his New York paper, describing his financial lot as he begged his debtors to pay up: "My every day [clothes] are almost worn out. [Please] send the poor printer a few gammons [slabs of bacon], or some meal, some butter, cheese, poultry."[54]

Boston printer Thomas Fleet explained his financial situation in a similar newspaper advertisement: "It is well-known that we are the most Humble, self-denying Set of Mortals . . . breathing; for where there is a penny to be got, we readily resign it up to those who are in no ways related to the business, nor have any Pretence or Claim to the Advantages of it."[55]

Most printers preferred to pursue outside ventures rather than beg for money, however. Some acted as merchants, selling molasses, sugar, rice, and even pewter. Sower and Thomas operated their own paper mills, and Sower's son, Christopher Jr., who was also a printer, made and sold type. A number of printers, including Franklin, served as postmasters for their communities.

As purveyors of intellectual discourse and information, printers occupied a special niche among craftsmen. They played a particularly important role during the Revolution, publishing news about the war's progress as well as those who supported the birth of a new nation. It is no wonder, then, that printers like Thomas looked back on their careers with such pride. "My attachment to the art [of printing], of which we are professors, is not diminished," Thomas wrote when he was in his seventies. "Could I live my life over again and choose my employment, it would be that of Printer."[56]

CRAFTSMEN AND THE NATION

Many craftsmen fought in the American Revolution, and even those who did not serve in the military made significant contributions to the birth of the new nation. Blacksmiths, for example, forged the building nails and plows that helped keep colonists housed and fed as the new American society began to grow and flourish. Gunsmiths forged the rifles American soldiers took into battle. Silversmiths created some of the nation's first works of art and helped keep its wealth safe. Wig makers served America's new merchant and professional class, and printers published the information that sparked a revolution and nurtured a culture. Thus every craftsman, no matter how great or humble, made a contribution to the new nation that was America.

NOTES

CHAPTER 1:
BECOMING A CRAFTSMAN

1. Quoted in Henry J. Kauffman, *The Colonial Silversmith: His Techniques and His Products.* Camden, NJ: Thomas Nelson, 1969, p. 43.
2. Quoted in Thomas Fleming, *Benjamin Franklin: A Biography in His Own Words.* New York: Harper & Row, 1972, p. 20.
3. Quoted in Fleming, *Benjamin Franklin*, p. 19.
4. Quoted in John Woodforde, *The Strange Story of False Hair.* New York: Drake, 1972, p. 61.
5. Quoted in Esther Forbes, *Paul Revere and the World He Lived In.* Cambridge, MA: Riverside, 1942, p. 9.
6. Forbes, *Paul Revere and the World He Lived In*, p. 22.
7. Aldren A. Watson, *The Village Blacksmith.* New York: Thomas Y. Crowell, 1968, p. 34.

CHAPTER 2: THE BLACKSMITH

8. Watson, *The Village Blacksmith*, p. 93.
9. Scott G. Williamson, *The American Craftsman.* New York: Crown, 1940, p. 134.
10. Watson, *The Village Blacksmith*, p. 13.
11. Watson, *The Village Blacksmith*, p. 1.
12. Watson, *The Village Blacksmith*, p. 38.
13. Watson, *The Village Blacksmith*, p. 50.
14. Watson, *The Village Blacksmith*, p. 75.
15. Edwin Tunis, *Colonial Craftsmen and the Beginnings of American Industry.* Baltimore, MD: Johns Hopkins University Press, 1965, pp. 58, 60.
16. Quoted in Watson, *The Village Blacksmith*, p. 2.

CHAPTER 3: THE GUNSMITH

17. Quoted in Hans Tanner, ed., *Guns of the World.* New York: Bonanza, 1972, p. 7.
18. Tanner, *Guns of the World*, p. 8.
19. Tanner, *Guns of the World*, p. 16.
20. Merrill Lindsay, *The Kentucky Rifle.* New York: Arma, 1972, p. 11.
21. Tunis, *Colonial Craftsmen and the Beginnings of American Industry*, p. 64.
22. Tanner, *Guns of the World*, p. 12.
23. Tanner, *Guns of the World*, pp. 11–12.

CHAPTER 4: THE SILVERSMITH

24. Kauffman, *The Colonial Silversmith*, p. 21.

25. Quoted in John Marshall Phillips, *American Silver.* Mineola, NY: Dover, 2001, p. 111.
26. Quoted in Graham Hood, *American Silver: A History of Style.* New York: Praeger, 1971, p. 18.
27. Hood, *American Silver*, p. 18.
28. Quoted in Martha Gandy Fales, *Early American Silver for the Cautious Collector.* New York: Funk & Wagnalls, 1970, p. 28.
29. Williamson, *The American Craftsman*, p. 112.
30. Quoted in Fales, *Early American Silver for the Cautious Collector*, p. 203.
31. Kauffman, *The Colonial Silversmith*, p. 35.
32. Kauffman, *The Colonial Silversmith*, p. 33.
33. Forbes, *Paul Revere and the World He Lived In*, p. 22.
34. Quoted in Kauffman, *The Colonial Silversmith*, p. 35.
35. Quoted in Kauffman, *The Colonial Silversmith*, p. 36.
36. Quoted in Forbes, *Paul Revere and the World He Lived In*, p. 126.
37. Quoted in Kauffman, *The Colonial Silversmith*, p. 38.
38. Williamson, *The American Craftsman*, p. 114.
39. Quoted in Kauffman, *The Colonial Silversmith*, p. 45.

CHAPTER 5: THE WIG MAKER

40. Quoted in *The Wigmaker in Eighteenth-Century Williamsburg: An Account of His Barbering, Hair-Dressing, and Peruke-Making Services, and Some Remarks on Wigs of Various Styles.* Williamsburg, VA: Colonial Williamsburg Foundation, 1979, p. 10.
41. Quoted in *The Wigmaker in Eighteenth-Century Williamsburg*, p. 11.
42. Quoted in *The Wigmaker in Eighteenth-Century Williamsburg*, p. 28.
43. Tunis, *Colonial Craftsmen and the Beginnings of American Industry*, p. 43.

CHAPTER 6: THE PRINTER

44. Isaiah Thomas, *The History of Printing in America.* New York: Weathervane, 1970, p. 63.
45. Quoted in Edith Merwin Bartow, *News and These United States.* New York: Funk & Wagnalls, 1952, p. 21.
46. Tunis, *Colonial Craftsmen and the Beginnings of American Industry*, p. 127.
47. Tunis, *Colonial Craftsmen and the Beginnings of American Industry*, p. 127.
48. Williamson, *The American Craftsman*, p. 150.
49. Quoted in Joseph Blumenthal, *The Printed Book in America.* Boston: David R. Godine, 1977, p. 6.
50. Lawrence C. Wroth, *The Colonial Printer.* Charlottesville, VA: Dominion, 1964, p. 229.
51. Wroth, *The Colonial Printer*, p. 230.

52. Quoted in Blumenthal, *The Printed Book in America*, p. 4.
53. Wroth, *The Colonial Printer*, p. 227.
54. Quoted in Frank Luther Mott, *American Journalism*. New York: Macmillan, 1962, p.
55. Quoted in Thomas, *The History of Printing in America*, p. 3.
56. Quoted in Blumenthal, *The Printed Book in America*, p. 23.

FOR FURTHER READING

BOOKS

Leonard Everett Fisher, *The Wigmakers*. New York: Benchmark, 1965. Fisher's book, written for young people, offers a clear account of the wig-making process and the craftsmen who pursued it.

Benjamin Franklin, *The Autobiography of Benjamin Franklin*. Ed. Leonard W. Labaree. New Haven, CT: Yale University Press, 1964. Advanced readers will enjoy Franklin's story in his own words. Franklin briefly covers his childhood and his earliest days in the printing trade, which he entered rather unwillingly but eventually embraced as part of his natural literary bent.

Augusta Stevens, *Paul Revere: Boston Patriot*. New York: Aladdin Library, 1986. This book for young people is a colorful, well-told story of Revere's life and career, not only as a silversmith but as a patriot and statesman.

Millicent Stow, *American Silver*. New York: Gramercy, 1950. This short book gives a brief history of silversmiths and their craftsmanship. But its true focus is pictures, and there is no better way to appreciate the artistry of America's smiths than to see it firsthand.

Edwin Tunis, *Colonial Living*. New York: Thomas Y. Crowell, 1976. Tunis is the author of several books on colonial and frontier life. *Colonial Living* details the day-to-day life of the colonists and provides a good deal of information on the crafts that flourished in the home throughout the colonial period.

Kathy Wilmore, *A Day in the Life of a Colonial Blacksmith*. New York: PowerKids, 2000. Wilmore's book details the workday of a hypothetical colonial blacksmith. Although written for young readers, the book gives a precise detailing of the smith's tools, his customers, and how he makes his products.

———, *A Day in the Life of a Colonial Wigmaker*. New York: PowerKids, 2000. Wilmore gives the same treatment to the wig maker, detailing his products, customers, services, and prices. She also includes a list of Internet sources for those who want to further research this craft.

Benjamin Labaree Woods, *The Boston Tea Party*. New York: New York University Press, 1964. There are many easy-to-read books on the Boston Tea Party, but young readers who like a challenge will enjoy this one. It examines the issues behind the event, the event's aftermath, and the perpetrators who actually threw the tea.

WEB SITES

Colonial Williamsburg (www.history. org). Williamsburg has a wealth of information on colonial life, and this general Web site is a good introduction. In addition to resources on colonial life, the site includes information on the many craft re-creations that exist in the village itself. "Craftsmen" ply their trades and answer questions about them for visitors. The site also directs the visitor to various Web pages that offer short descriptions of the crafts of silversmithing, wig making, blacksmithing, and gunsmithing.

Kentucky Long Rifle (www.frontier folk.org/ky-lr.htm). This Web site offers not only a history of the Kentucky rifle but information on flintlocks, frontier life, military life, and various organizations that offer frontier reenactments. The site is very user friendly, offers plenty of links, and is well illustrated.

WORKS CONSULTED

BOOKS

Edith Merwin Bartow, *News and These United States*. New York: Funk & Wagnalls, 1952. Bartow's book focuses more on the history of journalism than on the trade of printing. However, she does include information on the travails of early printers who doubled as newspaper publishers and braved the wrath of the Crown when their editorial content did not fit British standards.

Joseph Blumenthal, *The Printed Book in America*. Boston: David R. Godine, 1977. Blumenthal takes a look at not only the history of the book but the history of printing in America. His work details early books, early printers, and bookbinders, both in the colonial period and beyond.

Carl Bridenbaugh, *The Colonial Craftsman*. New York: New York University Press, 1950. Bridenbaugh's book on colonial crafts looks at the big picture. He details the growth of crafts and the arrival of craftsmen in the northern, middle, and southern colonies. He pinpoints which crafts sprung up in which regions, and when, and how these crafts served individual cities and communities.

David F. Butler, *The American Shotgun.* New York: Winchester, 1973. Butler's focus is on American weapons only, and he includes details on the making of guns, particularly the flintlock component, and the development of the Kentucky rifle.

S.E. Ellacott, *Guns.* London: Methuen, 1955. This book is fairly short, but gives a good overview of the history of guns, how they changed and developed, and their use in Europe and America. It also puts the use of weapons in colonial America in a historical context.

Martha Gandy Fales, *Early American Silver for the Cautious Collector.* New York: Funk & Wagnalls, 1970. Fales's book focuses not only on silver-making techniques but on the quirkier side of silver making (and silver owning) during the colonial era.

Thomas Fleming, *Benjamin Franklin: A Biography in His Own Words.* New York: Harper & Row, 1972. Fleming uses Franklin's own unfinished autobiography as his basis and fills in the blanks of Franklin's remarkable life. He spends a fair amount of time on Franklin's early life, as well as that of his candle-maker father, and his first years in the printing trade.

Esther Forbes, *Paul Revere and the World He Lived In.* Cambridge, MA: Riverside, 1942. Forbes's prose is rather flowery and difficult to read, but she goes on at length about Revere's French Huguenot father, Appollos; his arrival in America; and his apprenticeship to John Coney. She also details Revere's early years in his father's silversmith shop and the daily life of a smith.

Ian V. Hogg, *The Story of the Gun.* New York: St. Martin's, 1996. Unlike many books on colonial firearms, Hogg's focus is not only the Kentucky rifle. He also discusses the French rifle and English Brown Bess that were in use during the era and repaired by colonial gunsmiths.

Graham Hood, *American Silver: A History of Style.* New York: Praeger, 1971. Hood's book focuses more on the product than the craftsmanship, but he does provide a good sense of a society that turned its coins into artwork. Hood also includes many pictures depicting colonial silver.

Henry J. Kauffman, *The Colonial Silversmith: His Techniques and His Products.* Camden, NJ: Thomas Nelson, 1969. Kauffman's emphasis is on the making of silver, describing in great detail the silversmith's tools, techniques, and designs. A good resource for the student looking to find out more about the old-fashioned art of silversmithing. Kauffman also provides black-and-white photographs of some examples of America's oldest silver plate.

Merrill Lindsay, *The Kentucky Rifle.* New York: Arma, 1972. Those interested in the Kentucky rifle will enjoy this short book, which provides detailed descriptions of the gun and its makers. It also includes photographs of surviving examples of the rifle.

Frank Luther Mott, *American Journalism.* New York: Macmillan, 1962. Mott's emphasis is on colonial journalism and newspapers, but he discusses the role of the printer as journalist, the courageous stance that many early printers took, and the role of the press in the American Revolution.

National Geographic Society, *The Craftsman in America.* Washington, DC: National Geographic Society, 1975. This book is a compilation of *National Geographic* magazine articles on the American craftsman by various authors. The information covers the colonial period and beyond, including modern-day craft making, exploring how today's craftsmen strive to keep time-honored techniques alive.

John Marshall Phillips, *American Silver.* Mineola, NY: Dover, 2001. Phillips discusses the role of silver in society, how it cemented families and preserved the family's heritage, not to mention its wealth, and how silver was made. Silver was exchanged at weddings, funerals, the births of children, and at nearly every other major life event.

Bill Severn, *The Long and Short of It: Five Thousand Years of Fun and Fury over Hair.* New York: David McKay, 1971. Severn includes a chapter on colonial wig making, but his true emphasis is worldwide: the history of hairstyles, hairpieces, and wigs dating back to ancient times.

Hans Tanner, ed., *Guns of the World.* New York: Bonanza, 1972. Tanner's focus is international, but he includes an excellent chapter on the Kentucky rifle, detailing its construction and the battles in which it played a key role.

Isaiah Thomas, *The History of Printing in America.* New York: Weathervane, 1970. Thomas was a contemporary of Benjamin Franklin, and his *History of Printing* originally appeared in 1810. His writing style is quite formal and dry, considering the fact that he knew most of his subjects; he even refers to himself in the third person. But he does include complete biographies of every colonial printer, as well as a discussion of the trade itself.

Edwin Tunis, *Colonial Craftsmen and the Beginnings of American Industry.* Baltimore, MD: Johns Hopkins University Press, 1965. This book takes a broad view of almost every kind of craft and craftsman in the colonial period, from printer to blacksmith to wig maker. Tunis includes great detail on craft technique and products.

Aldren A. Watson, *The Village Blacksmith.* New York: Thomas Y. Crowell, 1968. Watson discusses the work of the blacksmith in the seventeenth, eighteenth, and nineteenth centuries. He includes very useful details on techniques at the forge and anvil, and the many products a blacksmith produced.

The Wigmaker in Eighteenth-Century Williamsburg: An Account of His Barbering, Hair-Dressing, and Peruke-Making Services, and Some Remarks on Wigs of Various Styles. Williamsburg, VA: Colonial Williamsburg Foundation, 1979. The Colonial Williamsburg Foundation publishes a good deal of material on the many crafts represented in its colonial village. This pamphlet contains a very detailed description of the wig-making process, step by step, from start to finish.

Scott G. Williamson, *The American Craftsman.* New York: Crown, 1940. This book includes chapters on blacksmithing, gunsmithing, printing, and silversmithing, as well as some of the more obscure crafts like pottery and leatherwork. Williamson also spotlights some of the more significant craftsmen in colonial history, such as silversmiths John Coney and Samuel Casey and printer Isaiah Thomas.

John Woodforde, *The Strange Story of False Hair.* New York: Drake, 1972. Woodforde's chapter on wigs in the colonial era describes the attitudes and opinions toward wig wearing, as well as the styles and fashions of the day. The chapter lists some wig-making techniques and provides graphic depictions of wig makers' tools.

Lawrence C. Wroth, *The Colonial Printer.* Charlottesville, VA: Dominion, 1964. This book is extremely dry and technical in parts, but it includes complete descriptions of colonial printing machinery, type, paper, wages, working conditions, and important printers of the day. It also details various publications of the colonial era, including almanacs, newspapers, and various magazines.

PERIODICAL

Joseph Judge, "Williamsburg, City of All Seasons," *National Geographic*, December 1968.

INTERNET SOURCES

Ed Crews, "The Gunsmith's Shop," *Journal of the Colonial Williamsburg Foundation*, Autumn 2000. www.history.org/foundation/journal/Autumn00/gunsmith.cfm.

Graham Ford, "Phlebotomy: The Ancient Art of Bloodletting," www.mtn.org/quack/devices/phlebo.htm.

George Hewes, "The Boston Tea Party: Eyewitness Account by a Participant," www.historyplace.com/unitedstates/revolution/teaparty.htm.

INDEX

in # # # # # itle

silver wire, 61–62
skillets (silversmithing tools), 56
sled runners, 32
smithy, 27–28
smoothbore muskets, 44, 49
snipers, 42
social status, 10, 65
 of blacksmiths, 24, 36, 38
 of gunsmiths, 39, 50
 of printers, 78, 81
 of silversmiths, 53–54, 64, 76
 of wig makers, 66
soldering process, 58–59, 62
South America, 54
Sower, Christopher, 81, 91
Spain, 54
steel, 44–46
stocks, gun, 39, 41, 43, 46–49
stonemen (printers), 83
strikers (blacksmiths), 23–24, 32
Sweden, 27

tavern owners, 25, 36
taxes, 11, 29
teapots, 58–59
tempering process, 32–35, 45–46, 57–58
Thomas, Isaiah, 18, 78, 88, 91

tools, 10
 of blacksmiths, 28–32
 for bloodletting, 75
 of gunsmiths, 43–44
 of printers, 82–85
 of silversmiths, 54–56
 of wig makers, 68, 70
tooth pulling, 70, 73
trades, learning of, 13–24
tradesmen, 75
training, 13–24
Tye wigs, 75–76
tympans, 84–85
type, printers', 82

urban areas, 38–39, 46, 50, 65, 81

Vermont, 27
Virginia, 27, 42
 see also Williamsburg, Virginia

wages, 21–22
Washington, George, 56
wealthy people, 10–11, 51–54, 61–63, 65–66, 73–75, 77
weather vanes, 36
weaving, of hair, 71
welts (wig making), 71–72

PICTURE CREDITS

ABOUT THE AUTHOR

Mary C. Wilds's latest book for Lucent is *The Indigenous Peoples of Indonesia.* She is also the author of *The Indigenous Peoples of Southeast Asia* and *The Shawnee*, as well as a four-book black history series for Avisson Press. Her stage plays, *Looking at You, Kid* and *The Fourth House*, have been produced in Los Angeles, San Luis Obispo, and Cambria, California.